Get A Life - Get The Life You Really Want

Brian McGinty

Published by Brian McGinty, 2024.

While every precaution has been taken in the preparation of this book, the publisher assumes no responsibility for errors or omissions, or for damages resulting from the use of the information contained herein.

GET A LIFE - GET THE LIFE YOU REALLY WANT

First edition. March 22, 2024.

Copyright © 2024 Brian McGinty.

ISBN: 979-8224084869

Written by Brian McGinty.

Also by Brian McGinty

Unleashing Your Infinite Potential
Get A Life - Get The Life You Really Want

Watch for more at https://getalife.info.

Table of Contents

To my darling wife Emma and my children, Caogáin,
Emily, Bryony and Jimmy.

Table of Contents

Gratitude

Practicing presence and appreciation for a balanced and fulfilling life.

10. **Chapter 9: The Principle of Service**

Giving back and helping others as a foundation for a meaningful existence.

11. **Chapter 10: The Principle of Financial Intelligence**

Managing and investing wisely for long-term prosperity and freedom.

12. **Chapter 11: The Principle of Goal Setting and Visualization**

Defining aspirations and using visualization to bring goals to fruition.

13. **Chapter 12: The Principle of Personal Power and Action**

Unleashing potential and taking proactive steps towards achieving desired outcomes.

Conclusion: The Path Forward

Reflecting on the transformation undergone, and looking ahead to implementing the principles in daily life.

Acknowledgements

Expressing gratitude to those who have inspired and supported this project.

About the Author

A brief biography of Brian McGinty, highlighting his life, qualifications, and vision for helping others "Get A Life" they love.

Introduction

A Personal Transformation

Welcome to "Get A Life" — a manifesto and a guide born from my own journey of self-discovery, challenge, and transformation. My name is Brian McGinty, I am 46 years old, and from a small village called Ballindrait, in the northwest of Ireland. I have been happily married to Emma for ten years and have four children, Caogain, Emily Bryony and Jimmy and we live in a beautiful villa overlooking the Mediterranean in Malta.

Over the past ten years, I've embarked on a quest not just to improve my life but to understand the underlying principles that dictate our paths to fulfilment, happiness, and purpose. This book is a culmination of that voyage, an amalgamation of personal experiences, extensive reading, and dedicated research.

Why I Wrote This Book

My path to writing this book did not stem from a tale of triumph but rather from a stark realization: I was not living the life I had once dreamt for myself. Like so many others, I encountered personal and professional obstacles that appeared too daunting to overcome.

The year 2013 marked a particularly low point: no home, no car, zero finances for food or rent. In the years preceding, Emma lost her mother to cancer at the young age of 53, her grandmother passed away, and my own mother was battling dementia. Emma, having spent seven years as a missionary in Tanzania, was grappling with chronic fatigue and was now expecting. Amidst this, I had lost my business. With Emma unable to work and me unable to leave her side to go to work, compounded by the lack of government support in a foreign country, our situation seemed dire.

Yet, it was within these depths of despair that I unearthed the strength of resilience, the necessity for growth, and the life-changing potential of a mindset focused on continual self-improvement—not out of desire, but from a lack of alternatives.

A pivotal moment arrived when a friend, recognizing our plight, recommended "Think and Grow Rich" by Napoleon Hill. My initial response was dismissive—I needed financial relief, not literary inspiration, and laughed at the idea of spending €10 I didn't have on a book, especially given my history of struggling with concentration and reading.

Undeterred, he suggested the audiobook version, enticing me by mentioning Henry Ford, and the fact that the first Audible book was free. This suggestion marked the beginning of a transformational period in my life and ignited a deep-seated gratitude for my friend's insistence.

In the years that followed, I delved into the teachings of renowned thinkers like Wallace Wattles, James Allen, Earl Nightingale, Bob Proctor, Tony Robbins, and George S. Clason. These explorations did more than offer guidance; they sparked a mission to impart these enduring principles to others.

My credentials to author this book don't come adorned with academic honours but are deeply rooted in the practical application of the principles I've lived and now share. In a world awash with information yet still facing widespread dissatisfaction and financial insecurity, it's clear that education alone isn't the panacea it was once thought to be. True power lies not in mere knowledge but in the application of that knowledge through action.

My educational journey has since been enriched by formal qualifications as a Professional Life Coach, a Certified Belief Clearing Practitioner, and a Certified Mentor under Bob Proctor's guidance. Yet, these titles are not where my true strength lies. My lived experiences, the victories I've claimed, and the lessons learned along the way are what truly qualify me to guide others on their path to "Get A Life" that's not just endured, but fully embraced and enjoyed.

The Essence of This Book

This is not meant to be a collection of abstract principles but a practical guide designed to walk you through the process of transforming your life from the ordinary to the extraordinary. It distils wisdom from a wide array of sources, bringing together insights on resilience, authenticity, financial intelligence, and the art of leaving a lasting legacy.

What You Can Expect

As you explore this book, you'll find not just a reflection of my life but a mirror for your own aspirations and challenges. This book is structured to provide you with actionable strategies, reflective exercises, and real-life examples that demonstrate the power of these principles in action.

- You'll learn how to embrace challenges as opportunities for growth, drawing from my own experiences of overcoming adversity and leveraging setbacks as catalysts for advancement.

- I'll share with you the importance of authenticity in forging deep connections and leading a life aligned with your true values, informed by my journey towards living more authentically and the impact it has had on my relationships and career.
- Together, we'll explore the principles of financial intelligence, inspired by my own path to understanding and managing wealth, guided by the lessons learned from masters of financial strategy and personal finance.
- You'll discover the significance of crafting a legacy that transcends material wealth, reflecting on my aspirations to leave behind a world enriched by my contributions and how you can do the same.

Join Me

This book is an invitation to you, the reader, to join me on this road because I am still on it myself. Success is not a destination; in Earl Nightingales' words "Success is the progressive realisation of a worthy ideal"

I can give you a promise that, no matter where you're starting from, the principles contained within these pages can guide you to a life of greater purpose, joy, and fulfilment. I will be with you every step of the way, sharing insights, the lessons I've learned, and the strategies that have propelled me forward.

Embarking Together

With each principle, story, and lesson, I invite you to reflect, engage, and apply these teachings to your life, confident in the knowledge that transformation is not only possible but within your reach. Welcome to "Get A Life" — your guide to unlocking the extraordinary within the ordinary, led by someone who has walked the path and is committed to helping you achieve the very same.

Chapter 1: The Principle of Self-Mastery

Unlocking Your Potential

The road to a fulfilled life begins with the mastery of one's self. Self-mastery, the art of controlling your thoughts, emotions, and actions, is the foundation upon which all personal achievements are built. It's a principle that echoes through the teachings of many great thinkers and is the bedrock of any transformational journey.

The Genesis of Change: Thought

Everything starts with a thought. This simple yet profound truth underpins the principle of self-mastery. Our thoughts are the architects of our destiny, shaping our perceptions, actions, and ultimately, our reality. James Allen's timeless insight in "As a Man Thinketh" illuminates this concept: our life is the direct result of our thoughts. If we sow seeds of positivity and purpose in our mental garden, we reap the fruits of success and happiness.

Cultivating Awareness

The first step toward self-mastery is cultivating a deep awareness of our thoughts. It requires us to become vigilant gardeners of our minds, discerning which thoughts contribute to our growth and which serve only to entangle us in the weeds of negativity and doubt.

This cultivation begins with mindfulness, the practice of observing our thoughts and emotions without judgment. Mindfulness teaches us that we are not our thoughts; we are the observer of our thoughts. This realization is

empowering—it means we have the choice to water the seeds of positive thoughts and uproot the weeds of destructive ones.

Exercises for Enhancing Self-Awareness:

1. **Daily Reflection:** Dedicate time each day to reflect on your thoughts and emotions. Journaling can be a powerful tool for this practice, helping you identify patterns and triggers in your thought process.

2. **Mindful Breathing:** Engage in mindful breathing exercises. Focus solely on the rhythm of your breath to bring yourself into the present moment, creating a space of clarity and calmness from which to observe your thoughts.

3. **Question Your Thoughts:** Challenge your negative thoughts by asking yourself, "Is this thought true? Is it helpful? Does it lead me towards the life I want to create?" This practice can help shift your thought patterns towards more positive and constructive ones.

Discipline: The Pillar of Self-Mastery

With awareness comes the ability to discipline our thoughts. Discipline in this context is not about restriction but about alignment—aligning our thoughts with our values and goals. It involves choosing to focus on thoughts that empower us and move us closer to our aspirations.

Building Positive Habits

Self-mastery extends beyond thought into action. The habits we cultivate play a pivotal role in this transformation. As James Clear articulates in "Atomic Habits," small, consistent actions lead to significant changes. By focusing on building positive habits, we create a framework for success that operates even when our motivation wanes.

Starting Small:

1. **The Two-Minute Rule:** If a task takes less than two minutes, do it immediately. This rule helps overcome procrastination and lays the groundwork for more significant habits.
2. **Habit Stacking:** Link a new habit to an existing routine. For example, if you wish to practice gratitude, take a moment to think of three things you're grateful for every morning as you drink your coffee.

As we delve deeper into the principle of self-mastery, remember that mastery of anything requires continuous growth and learning. The path is not always linear, and setbacks are part of the process. However, with each step forward, you gain greater insight into your inner workings and move closer to the life you envision.

Navigating the Landscape of Emotions

A critical aspect of self-mastery involves navigating the complex landscape of our emotions. Emotional intelligence, the ability to identify, understand, and manage our own emotions and the emotions of others, is pivotal. It enables us to respond to life's situations with wisdom rather than being hijacked by fleeting feelings. This skill fosters resilience, enhancing our ability to face challenges and bounce back from setbacks.

Enhancing Emotional Intelligence:

1. **Emotional Awareness:** Start by recognizing your emotions as they arise. Naming your emotions can be a powerful step towards understanding them.
2. **Emotional Regulation:** Learn techniques to calm intense emotions. Deep breathing, meditation, or even taking a walk can help shift your emotional state.
3. **Empathetic Listening:** Improve your relationships by practising empathetic listening. This involves truly hearing what the other person is saying without immediately formulating a response or judgment.

The Symphony of Self-Talk

The dialogue we have with ourselves, our self-talk, plays a monumental role in shaping our reality. Negative self-talk can be a critical barrier to self-mastery, reinforcing self-doubt and limiting beliefs. Conversely, positive self-talk acts as a catalyst for growth and confidence. Changing this internal narrative is a powerful step toward mastering oneself.

Strategies for Positive Self-Talk:

- **Affirmations:** Use affirmations to reinforce positive beliefs about yourself. These should be present tense, positive statements that resonate with your goals and values.
- **Cognitive Restructuring:** Challenge and change negative thought patterns. When you catch yourself in a cycle of negative self-talk, pause and ask, "Is this

thought accurate? Is there a more positive and realistic way to view this situation?"

The Strength of Willpower and Discipline

Willpower and discipline are often viewed as the muscles of self-mastery; they enable us to persist in our efforts even when faced with temptation or fatigue. However, it's crucial to understand that willpower is not infinite—it can be depleted. Therefore, creating an environment that reduces the need for willpower and enhances discipline is essential.

Techniques to Strengthen Willpower:

- **Simplify Choices:** Reduce the number of decisions you need to make each day. This can help conserve willpower for the tasks that truly matter.
- **Reward System:** Create a reward system for yourself. Small rewards for completing tasks or maintaining discipline can provide motivation and satisfaction.

The Ritual of Routine

Routines are the scaffolding of self-mastery, providing structure and predictability that pave the way for progress. By establishing routines around your most important tasks and goals, you automate progress, making success a part of your daily life.

Building Effective Routines:

- **Morning Ritual:** Start your day with a ritual that sets the tone for success. This could include exercise, meditation, reading, or any activity that energizes and focuses you.

- **Evening Reflection:** End your day with a routine of reflection. Review what went well, what could be improved, and how you can make tomorrow better.

The Art of Adaptability

Self-mastery is not just about rigid control but also about adaptability—being able to adjust to changing circumstances while maintaining focus on your goals. This flexibility is crucial in a world that is constantly changing.

Cultivating Adaptability:

- **Embrace Change:** View change as an opportunity for growth. When faced with new challenges, ask yourself what you can learn from the experience.
- **Stay Curious:** Maintain a mindset of curiosity. This openness can help you adapt more easily to new situations and find creative solutions to problems.

Mindfulness: The Anchor of Self-Mastery

Mindfulness, the practice of being present and fully engaged in the current moment without judgment, is the anchor of self-mastery. It brings awareness to our thoughts, emotions, and actions, allowing us to live more intentionally.

Practising Mindfulness:

- **Daily Meditation:** Incorporate meditation into your daily routine. Even a few minutes can increase mindfulness, reduce stress, and improve focus.
- **Mindful Activities:** Engage in activities mindfully,

whether eating, walking, or listening. Fully immerse yourself in the experience, paying attention to the senses and emotions involved.

As we walk down the path of self-mastery, remember that each step, no matter how small, is a step towards the person you aspire to be. This middle segment of our exploration into self-mastery has delved into emotional intelligence, the power of self-talk, the importance of discipline and willpower, the structuring force of routine, the necessity of adaptability, and the grounding practice of mindfulness. Each of these aspects intertwines to form the intricate tapestry of self-mastery, guiding us towards a life of purpose, fulfilment, and achievement.

As we approach the culmination of this chapter, it's essential to recognize that this journey is both deeply personal and universally relevant. The final pieces of the puzzle involve integrating our insights into daily life and understanding the cyclical nature of growth and mastery.

Integration: Living Your Mastery

The true test of self-mastery isn't found in isolated moments of discipline or flashes of insight but in the consistent application of these principles in our daily lives. Integration means taking the lessons of mindfulness, emotional intelligence, discipline, and adaptability, and weaving them into the fabric of our everyday experiences.

Strategies for Integration:

- **Set Clear Intentions:** Begin each day by setting clear intentions. What do you wish to achieve? How do you want to feel? Intentions act as a compass, guiding your actions and thoughts throughout the day.

- **Reflect and Adjust:** At the end of each day, take time to reflect on your experiences. What lessons did you learn? What could you improve? Reflection is a powerful tool for continuous growth.
- **Live Intentionally:** Make choices that align with your values and goals. Intentionality in your actions ensures that your life reflects your aspirations for mastery.

The Cycle of Growth

Understanding the cycle of growth is crucial for sustaining self-mastery. Growth is not a linear process but a cycle of expansion, contraction, learning, and integration. Embrace each phase of this cycle with openness and curiosity.

- **Expansion:** In this phase, you explore new concepts, challenge yourself, and step out of your comfort zone.
- **Contraction:** After expansion often comes contraction, a period of integration and reflection where growth may seem to slow.
- **Learning:** This phase is marked by the acquisition of new insights and understandings from the experiences of expansion and contraction.
- **Integration:** Finally, you integrate these learnings into your life, solidifying your growth and preparing for the next cycle.

Sustaining Your Mastery

Sustaining self-mastery over the long term requires patience, perseverance, and a commitment to continuous learning. Self-mastery is a lifelong pursuit, one that is constantly evolving as we grow and change.

- **Seek Support:** Surround yourself with a community that supports your growth. Whether through mentors, friends, or like-minded individuals, support is invaluable.
- **Stay Curious:** Maintain a mindset of lifelong learning. There is always something new to discover about ourselves and the world around us.
- **Celebrate Progress:** Take time to celebrate your achievements, no matter how small. Recognizing progress is essential for maintaining motivation and enthusiasm.

The Path Ahead

As we close this chapter on self-mastery, remember that this is just the beginning. The principles and practices discussed here are not merely steps to be checked off but layers to be explored and deepened over time. Self-mastery is about embracing the fullness of your potential, living with purpose, and making choices that reflect your highest self.

The path to self-mastery is both challenging and rewarding. It requires us to confront our limitations, to face our fears, and to step into our power. Yet, the rewards are immeasurable. Through self-mastery, we unlock the doors to a life of fulfilment, happiness, and true success.

As you move forward, carry with you the knowledge that self-mastery is within your reach. It is a path open to all who are willing to take action. With each step, you are not only transforming yourself but also shaping the world around you. The mastery of self is the most profound gift you can offer to yourself and to humanity.

Conclusion

This chapter has laid the foundation, offering tools and insights for mastering your thoughts, emotions, and actions. As you continue to apply these principles, remember that self-mastery is not a destination but a way of being. It is the art of living fully, embracing each moment with presence, purpose, and passion.

Let this chapter be a stepping stone on your path to "Get a Life" that resonates with your deepest aspirations. As you turn the pages of this book and the chapters of your life, know that self-mastery is one of the most rewarding journeys you will ever undertake.

Chapter 2: The Principle of Financial Intelligence

Financial Enlightenment

As we transition from mastering the self to mastering our finances, it's crucial to recognize that financial intelligence is not just about accumulating wealth—it's about understanding how money works and making it work for us. This road is one I've walked step by step, learning from both successes and setbacks. Robert Kiyosaki and George S Clason showed me the way, now, I aim to guide you through the landscape of financial intelligence, demystifying concepts and providing you with the tools to achieve your financial goals.

The Essence of Financial Intelligence

Financial intelligence begins with a fundamental shift in how we view money. It's not merely a means to an end but a tool for creating the life we desire. This shift in perspective is where true financial enlightenment starts. It's about understanding that financial success is not just about earning more but managing and growing what we have more effectively.

Understanding Your Financial Blueprint

Each of us has a financial blueprint, shaped by our upbringing, experiences, and beliefs about money. To develop financial intelligence, we must first become aware of this blueprint and recognize how it influences our financial decisions.

Ask yourself: What beliefs about money were instilled in me? Do these beliefs empower me or hold me back? This self-reflection is the first step towards rewriting your financial story.

Strategies for Enhancing Your Financial Blueprint:

- **Identify Limiting Beliefs:** Recognize any negative beliefs about money that may be limiting your financial potential. These could include notions like "money is the root of all evil" or "you have to work hard to make money."
- **Reframe Your Beliefs:** Begin to reframe these limiting beliefs into empowering ones. For instance, "Money is a tool for creating a positive impact" or "Wealth can be created through smart, informed decisions."
- **Change Your Language:** Swapping "I can't afford it," to "How can I afford it," instantly changed my mindset back in 2013 because it opened mental doors instead of closing them.

Budgeting: The Foundation of Financial Mastery

A budget is not just a record of income and expenses; it's a reflection of your values and priorities. Effective budgeting allows you to take control of your financial destiny, ensuring that your spending aligns with your goals.

Creating a Budget That Works for You:

1. **Track Your Spending:** For one month, keep a detailed record of all your spending. This exercise is eye-opening and provides a clear picture of where your money is going.

2. **Categorize Your Expenses:** Divide your expenses into categories (e.g., housing, food, transportation). This helps identify areas where adjustments can be made.
3. **Set Financial Goals:** Define clear, achievable financial goals. Whether it's saving for a down payment on a house, building an emergency fund, or investing in your education, having specific goals is motivating.

The Power of Saving and Investing

Saving is the process of setting aside money for future expenses or emergencies while investing is the act of using money to make more money. Both are critical components of financial intelligence.

Saving and Investing:

- **Pay Yourself First:** Before paying bills or making purchases, allocate a portion of your income to savings. Even a small amount, consistently saved, can grow significantly over time. Before you scream "I don't have anything left to save" think about what you would do if the government increased your income tax by 10%. Yes, exactly, you would pay for it. Pay yourself first and you will find that the other bills still get paid.
- **Explore Investment Options:** Educate yourself on investment options that align with your risk tolerance and financial goals. Whether it's stocks, bonds, crypto, wine, cars or real estate, understanding

the basics of investing is key to growing your wealth.

I also recommend investing in something you enjoy and have an interest in as learning about it will be more enjoyable. My interests include classic cars, gold and new technology so studying and investing in these areas has been fun and profitable.

Debt Management: Navigating the Path to Financial Freedom

Debt can be a significant barrier to financial freedom. Managing and reducing debt is an essential skill in your financial intelligence toolkit.

Effective Debt Management Strategies:

- **Prioritize High-Interest Debt:** Focus on paying off high-interest debt first, such as credit card balances, to reduce the amount of money paid in interest.
- **Consolidate Debts:** Consider consolidating multiple debts into a single loan with a lower interest rate. This can simplify payments and save money over time.

Cultivating Financial Literacy

Financial intelligence is built on a foundation of financial literacy—the understanding of financial principles and the ability to apply them to make informed decisions. Investing in your financial education is one of the most impactful steps you can take.

- **Read Financial Books:** Immerse yourself in the

wealth of knowledge found in financial books. Authors like Robert Kiyosaki and George S. Clason offer timeless wisdom on managing and growing wealth.

- **Attend Workshops and Seminars:** Participate in financial education workshops and seminars. These can provide valuable insights and networking opportunities.

This chapter is just the beginning of your quest for financial enlightenment, providing the foundational knowledge and actionable steps needed to take control of your financial future.

Navigating the complexities of financial intelligence requires more than just understanding the basics of budgeting, saving, and investing. It demands a deeper exploration into how we can optimize our financial resources to achieve lasting wealth and security. As we delve further into this chapter, let's explore advanced strategies for wealth building, the psychological aspects of financial decision-making, and how to create a robust financial plan that aligns with your life goals.

Advanced Strategies for Wealth Building

Once you've established a foundation of saving and investing, it's time to explore more sophisticated wealth-building strategies. This involves diversifying your investment portfolio, understanding the power of compound interest, and leveraging opportunities for passive income.

- **Diversification:** This strategy involves spreading your investments across various asset classes (e.g., stocks, bonds, metals, real estate) to reduce risk.

Diversification can protect your portfolio from volatility in any single investment or market sector.

- **Compound Interest:** Albert Einstein famously called compound interest "the eighth wonder of the world." It's the process by which a sum of money grows exponentially over time as interest earns interest. By starting early and investing regularly, you can harness the power of compound interest to build significant wealth.

- **Passive Income:** Explore avenues for generating income that don't require your active participation, such as rental properties, dividends from stocks, or creating and promoting digital products.

Throughout the past ten years, the creation and promotion of digital products have been instrumental in establishing my passive income streams. My preference leans strongly towards digital products for their inherent flexibility, not anchoring us to any single location. This mobility means that the dream of relocating, whether to a new city or a different country, becomes as simple as packing up my computer.

The essence of cultivating passive income streams lies in their ability to liberate time, enabling us to lead the lives we truly desire. They serve as the bedrock for "Getting A Life," providing the freedom to pursue our passions and enjoy life's moments fully.

This freedom has opened doors to spontaneous holidays, attending every school event without fail, and being present at home whenever life's small emergencies, like a sick child, arise. The value of time spent with family is immeasurable, a treasure that once passed, cannot be reclaimed. Hence, we cherish and maximize these moments, embracing the joys of life with our loved ones.

The Psychology of Money

Understanding the psychology behind your financial decisions is crucial to mastering financial intelligence. Our emotions and biases often influence our financial choices, sometimes to our detriment. Becoming aware of these psychological factors can help you make more rational and beneficial decisions.

- **Emotional Spending:** Recognize triggers that lead to impulsive buying or emotional spending. By identifying these triggers, you can develop strategies to avoid them, such as waiting 24 hours before making a purchase to ensure it aligns with your financial goals.
- **Overcoming Biases:** Humans are prone to cognitive biases that can skew our financial judgement, such as the confirmation bias (favouring information that confirms our existing beliefs) or the sunk cost fallacy (continuing a behaviour or endeavour as a result of previously invested resources). Being aware of these biases can help you make more objective decisions.

Creating a Financial Plan

A comprehensive financial plan is a roadmap for your financial future. It outlines your financial goals, strategies for achieving them, and how to manage risks along the way.

- **Set Specific, Measurable Goals:** Your financial goals should be specific (e.g., "create $10,000 for an emergency fund" rather than "save money") and measurable, with clear timelines for achievement. In my experience, creating your way to financial freedom is faster than trying to save your way there.

- **Assess Your Financial Situation:** Take a thorough inventory of your income, debts, expenses, and investments. This assessment provides a clear picture of where you stand and what steps you need to take to reach your goals.

- **Develop a Strategy:** Based on your goals and current financial situation, develop a strategy that includes budgeting, saving, investing, and debt management. Tailor your strategy to your unique circumstances and be prepared to adjust it as your financial situation evolves.

- **Manage Risks:** Consider potential financial risks, such as job loss or unexpected medical expenses, and plan accordingly. This could involve building a larger emergency fund or obtaining insurance coverage to protect against significant financial setbacks.

- **Regular Review and Adjustment:** Your financial plan is not set in stone. Regularly review and adjust your plan to reflect changes in your financial situation, goals, and priorities. This flexibility is key to staying on track towards your financial objectives.

As we explore financial intelligence, remember that the path to financial freedom is both a science and an art. It requires not only the knowledge of financial principles and strategies but also the wisdom to apply them in a way that aligns with your values and life goals. My experiences, both the triumphs and the challenges, have taught me that financial intelligence is within reach for anyone willing to learn, adapt, and persevere.

As we approach the conclusion, it's essential to recognize that knowledge alone isn't enough. True mastery comes from putting this knowledge into action and consistently refining our approach based on real-world experiences. Here, we'll focus on the practical application of your financial plan, effective tools for monitoring progress, and strategies to maintain motivation over the long haul.

Implementing Your Financial Plan

Taking the first step in implementing your financial plan can often be the most challenging. Start by prioritizing actions based on immediate impact and feasibility. For example, if high-interest debt is weighing you down, focusing on debt reduction strategies might be your first step. Alternatively, if you're relatively debt-free, beginning to invest or enhancing your investment strategy could be the starting point.

- **Automate Savings and Investments:** Automation is a powerful tool for maintaining discipline in savings and investments. Setting up automatic transfers to savings accounts or investment portfolios can help you stay consistent with your financial goals without having to think about it each month.

- **Reduce Expenses:** Look for areas where you can cut back without significantly impacting your quality of life. This might involve cancelling unused subscriptions, negotiating bills, or adopting more cost-effective habits.
- **Increase Income:** While reducing expenses is crucial, increasing your income can have an even more significant impact on your financial health. Consider side hustles, asking for a raise, or acquiring new skills that could lead to higher-paying opportunities. Looking back, I know that nothing really got better for me until I got better myself.

Tools for Monitoring Progress

Keeping a close eye on your financial health is essential for staying on course. Fortunately, numerous tools and resources can help you track your progress and make informed decisions.

- **Budgeting Apps:** Apps can help you manage your budget, track spending, and identify areas for improvement.
- **Investment Trackers:** Online trackers can provide a comprehensive view of your investment portfolio, performance analytics, and insights to inform your investment decisions.
- **Financial Planners:** For those who prefer a more personalized approach, a financial planner can offer tailored advice and strategies based on your unique financial situation and goals. Just remember not to

take advice from a poor Financial Advisor!

Staying Motivated

Maintaining motivation in the face of financial challenges or when goals seem distant is crucial. Here are some strategies to keep your spirits high and your focus sharp:

- **Celebrate Milestones:** Set mini-goals within your broader financial objectives and celebrate when you achieve them. This could be paying off a specific debt, reaching a savings target, or making your first investment.
- **Visualize Your Goals:** Keep a visual representation of your financial goals in a place where you'll see it daily. Whether it's a chart on your fridge or a vision board in your office, this reminder can help keep your goals top of mind.
- **Stay Educated:** Continue to educate yourself about financial matters. Reading books, listening to podcasts, and attending seminars can keep you informed and inspired.
- **Build a Support Network:** Surround yourself with people who share your financial aspirations. This community can offer encouragement, share insights, and help you stay on track.

The Path to Financial Mastery

Financial intelligence is about more than just accumulating wealth; it's about creating a life that aligns with your values, offers security and freedom, and enables you to make a positive impact on the world around you. By taking control of your finances, you're taking a significant step toward realizing your fullest potential. With commitment, education, and action, the path to financial mastery is within your reach.

Chapter 3: The Principle of Goal Setting and Visualization

Intention

"Get A Life" now guides us towards a crucial principle: the art of goal setting and visualization. This chapter delves into crafting a vision for your life that not only excites and motivates you but also is vividly brought to life through the power of visualization. Having navigated this path myself, I've witnessed the profound impact of setting clear, compelling goals and the dynamic changes that visualization can usher into our lives.

The Power of Clear Goals

The quest for personal transformation begins with clarity. Clear, well-defined goals serve as beacons, cutting through the fog of daily distractions and aligning your focus with your deepest aspirations. This clarity is not merely about knowing what you want; it's about understanding why you want it and how it aligns with your values and purpose in life.

Crafting Your Goals: A Step-by-Step Approach

1. **Define What You Truly Want:** Start with a period of reflection to discern what you genuinely desire. It's essential that these desires stem from your core values and vision for your life, not from external expectations or societal measures of success.

2. **Be Specific:** Ambiguity is the enemy of achievement. Specify your goals to ensure they are clear and actionable. Rather than saying, "I want to be wealthy," quantify what wealth means to you. How much

money do you aim to earn, save, or invest? What does achieving this level of financial security enable you to do?

3. **Write Them Down:** The simple act of writing down your goals moves them from the ephemeral realm of thought into tangible existence. Documenting your goals not only affirms your commitment to them but also serves as a constant reminder of what you're striving to achieve. My Mentor of ten years, Bob Proctor, introduced me to this concept and it did change my life.

4. **Set SMART Goals:** Adopt the SMART criteria—Specific, Measurable, Achievable, Relevant, Time-bound—to structure your goals. This approach imbues your objectives with clarity and feasibility, making it easier to monitor progress and adapt as necessary.

Visualization: Seeing Is Believing

Visualization transcends mere daydreaming; it's a strategic tool used by peak performers across various fields to enhance motivation and actualize their objectives. By vividly imagining the realization of your goals, you engage the brain's visual processing centres and the executive networks involved in planning and action, effectively preparing yourself to execute the steps required to achieve your goals.

Practical Exercises for Effective Visualization:

- **Daily Visualization Practice:** Allocate time each day for visualization. Envision your goals as already accomplished, immersing yourself in the details of this success. What does it look like? Who is with you? What emotions are you experiencing?

- **Create a Vision Board:** Assemble a vision board that visually represents your goals through images and words. This tangible representation of your aspirations serves as a daily visual cue, reinforcing your commitment and focus.
- **Use Affirmations:** Pair your visualization practice with positive affirmations that resonate with your goals. These affirmations should reinforce your belief in your ability to achieve what you visualize, creating a powerful synergy between thought and emotion.

The Role of Emotion in Visualization

The efficacy of visualization is significantly amplified by emotion. The feelings you associate with your visualized outcomes—joy, pride, gratitude—fuel your motivation and commitment. By emotionally engaging with your vision, you not only enhance the vividness of your visualizations but also align your subconscious mind with your goals, thereby activating your internal resources to make these visions a reality.

Personal Anecdotes: The Transformative Power of Goal Setting and Visualization

Through my own life, I've learned the invaluable role that goal setting and visualization play in achieving one's dreams. For instance, envisioning myself as a published author not only kept me anchored to my writing goals but also propelled me through the inevitable challenges and setbacks. This vision, rich in detail and emotion, became a north star, guiding my daily actions and decisions towards making that dream a reality.

Long before this, I had to visualise having €100 in my bank account, then having our own apartment, then a house, then a villa in the sun, and so my visualising continues. It is not a destination but an ever-changing, ever-evolving series of steps.

Embracing What Lies Ahead

As we progress through this chapter on goal setting and visualization, remember that the practices and principles shared here are more than just steps towards achieving specific outcomes. They are about aligning your life with your deepest values and aspirations, about transforming the vision of the life you desire into a tangible reality. Through the strategic application of goal setting and the power of visualization, you open yourself to a world of possibilities, setting the stage for a life that not only meets but exceeds your expectations.

Continuing our exploration into the transformative power of goal setting and visualization, we delve deeper into refining these practices, ensuring they are not just exercises but integral parts of a lifestyle geared towards achieving your dreams. This middle segment focuses on refining your visualization techniques, overcoming obstacles to your goals, and the importance of flexibility and adaptability in the goal-setting process.

Refining Visualization Techniques

Visualization is more than just seeing; it's about creating a sensory-rich experience in your mind. The more vividly you can imagine your success, the more real and attainable it feels. To refine your visualization, incorporate as many senses as you can. Imagine not just the sights but also the sounds, smells, and emotions associated with your success. If your goal is to run a marathon, don't just picture yourself crossing the finish line; hear the crowd cheering, feel the sweat on your brow, and the elation in your heart.

- **Regular Practice:** Like any skill, the effectiveness of visualization grows with practice. Dedicate time daily, even if just for a few minutes, to visualize your goals in detail. Morning or evening can be ideal times for this practice, allowing you to start or end your day aligned with your aspirations.
- **Visualization Meditation:** Incorporate visualization into a meditation practice. After achieving a relaxed state through breathing exercises, guide your focus towards visualizing your goals. This combination can be particularly powerful, as meditation helps clear the mind of distractions, enhancing the clarity and focus of your visualization.

Overcoming Obstacles

Few goals are achieved without obstacles. Anticipating these challenges and preparing for them is a crucial aspect of goal setting. Visualization can also be a tool here—envisioning yourself successfully navigating obstacles can prepare you mentally and emotionally for the challenges ahead.

- **Identify Potential Obstacles:** Reflect on what might hinder your progress towards your goals. These can be external, like financial constraints, or internal, like fear of failure. Acknowledging these potential roadblocks upfront can help you devise strategies to overcome them.

- **Develop Contingency Plans:** For each identified obstacle, develop a plan. If the obstacle is financial, your plan might involve setting aside a savings buffer or finding alternative funding sources. For internal obstacles, strategies might include seeking mentorship, additional training, or practising affirmations to bolster confidence.

The Importance of Flexibility and Adaptability

While having clear, specific goals is essential, so too is maintaining flexibility in how those goals are achieved. Life is dynamic, and circumstances can change, necessitating adjustments to our plans and even our goals themselves.

- **Stay Open to New Opportunities:** Sometimes, the pursuit of a goal can open unexpected doors. Be open to these opportunities, even if they weren't part of your original plan. They might lead to even greater achievements or fulfilment.
- **Regularly Review and Adjust Goals:** Set a regular schedule to review your goals and the progress towards them. This isn't just about tracking what you've achieved but also reassessing whether your goals still align with your values and long-term vision. As you grow and evolve, so too might your goals.

Sustaining Motivation

Maintaining motivation over the long term can be challenging, especially for goals that require sustained effort over months or years. Finding ways to keep your motivation high is crucial for long-term success.

- **Break Goals Down:** Large goals can be overwhelming. Break them down into smaller, manageable tasks or milestones. Achieving these smaller goals can provide a sense of progress and accomplishment, fueling your motivation to continue.
- **Seek Support:** Share your goals with friends, family, or a mentor. Having a support network can provide encouragement, advice, and accountability, helping you stay focused and motivated.
- **Celebrate Achievements:** Don't wait until you've reached your final goal to celebrate. Acknowledge and celebrate the completion of each step or milestone along the way. These celebrations can reinforce your commitment to your goals and provide the motivation to keep moving forward.

As we navigate the complexities of goal setting and visualization, remember that these are dynamic processes. They require not just initial enthusiasm but ongoing commitment, reflection, and adjustment. By regularly refining your techniques, preparing for obstacles, and maintaining flexibility and motivation, you set the stage for a journey not just towards achieving specific goals but towards a life of purpose, growth, and fulfilment.

In the final stretch of our exploration into goal setting and visualization, we focus on integrating these practices into a holistic approach to achieving your dreams. This involves understanding the symbiotic relationship between goal setting and visualization, leveraging community and accountability, and embracing it all with resilience and gratitude.

Integrating Goal Setting and Visualization

Integrating goal setting with visualization creates a powerful synergy that amplifies the effectiveness of both. While goal setting provides the roadmap, visualization fuels the emotional and psychological drive to navigate this road successfully. This integration involves a cyclical process of setting goals, visualizing outcomes, taking action, and reflecting on progress.

- **Actionable Visualization:** Ensure that your visualization practice includes actionable steps. Visualize not only the achievement of your goal but also the steps you took to get there. This approach bridges the gap between dreaming and doing, embedding the path to achievement within your visualization.

- **Align Visualization with Daily Actions:** Regularly align your daily actions with the outcomes you've visualized. This alignment ensures that your daily efforts are contributing directly to the realization of your visualized goals, keeping you consistently on track.

Leveraging Community and Accountability

Achieving your goals is often more rewarding and effective when shared. A community of like-minded individuals can provide support, inspiration, and a sense of belonging. Accountability, whether through a mentor, coach, or peer group, can significantly enhance your commitment and perseverance.

- **Find Your Tribe:** Seek out communities, both online and offline, that share your aspirations or have walked the path you're embarking on. These communities can be invaluable sources of knowledge, motivation, and support.
- **Establish Accountability Partnerships:** Pair up with someone who can hold you accountable to your goals. This partnership should be mutually supportive, providing a platform for sharing progress, challenges, and insights.

Resilience and Gratitude

Achieving meaningful goals is often a journey marked by highs and lows. Embracing these periods with resilience and gratitude enhances your ability to navigate challenges and celebrate successes.

- **Cultivate Resilience:** View setbacks as opportunities for growth. Developing a resilient mindset allows you to bounce back from challenges with increased strength and wisdom. Remember, resilience is not an innate trait but a skill that can be developed through practice and reflection.

- **Practice Gratitude:** Cultivate a habit of gratitude by regularly acknowledging and appreciating the progress you've made, the lessons learned and the support received. Gratitude not only enhances well-being but also puts challenges into perspective, fostering a positive outlook on what lies ahead.

Moving Forward with Purpose and Passion

As we conclude this chapter on goal setting and visualization, it's important to recognize that these principles are more than just tools for achieving specific objectives; they are foundational elements of a life lived with purpose and passion. The true power of goal setting and visualization lies in their ability to transform not only what you achieve but who you become in the process.

- **Reflect:** Take time to reflect on how the practice of goal setting and visualization has influenced your journey. What have you learned about yourself? How have your goals and aspirations evolved?
- **Stay Flexible and Open to Evolution:** Be open to the evolution of your goals as you grow and gain new insights. The path to fulfilment is not static but ever-changing, reflecting the continuous expansion of your horizons and understanding.
- **Embrace Each Step:** Celebrate every step, knowing that each action taken, challenge faced, and milestone achieved is shaping you into the person

you are meant to become.

By applying these principles with intention, discipline, and heart, you open the door to a life that is not only successful by your own definition but also rich in meaning and joy.

As you move forward, armed with the knowledge and practices shared in this chapter, know that the road toward your dreams is as unique and individual as you are. Embrace it with all its twists and turns, for it is in these experiences that the essence of life is truly found.

Chapter 4: The Principle of Continuous Learning and Adaptation

The Pathway to Growth and Evolution

In the unfolding narrative of "Get A Life," we now turn our focus to a principle that lies at the heart of personal and professional fulfilment: the principle of continuous learning and adaptation. This chapter is not merely an exploration of lifelong learning; it's a guide to cultivating a mindset that embraces growth, change, and the endless possibilities that come from remaining eternally curious and adaptable.

Cultivating a Growth Mindset

At the core of continuous learning is the concept of a growth mindset, a term coined by psychologist Carol Dweck. This mindset thrives on challenge and sees failure not as evidence of unintelligence but as a heartening springboard for growth and for stretching our existing abilities.

- **Embrace Challenges:** View challenges as opportunities to learn and grow rather than obstacles to avoid. Each challenge you overcome is a step forward in your personal development.
- **Learn from Criticism:** Constructive criticism is a valuable source of feedback. Learn to embrace it, analyze it, and use it to refine your skills and approaches.
- **Celebrate Effort, Not Just Success:** Recognize and celebrate the effort behind every achievement.

Understanding that success comes from hard work and perseverance is key to fostering a growth mindset.

The Power of Lifelong Learning

Lifelong learning is the deliberate pursuit of knowledge and skills throughout one's life. In today's rapidly changing world, the ability to learn and adapt is more critical than ever. Lifelong learners are more adaptable to change, better prepared for new opportunities, and more likely to find fulfilment and meaning in their personal and professional lives.

- **Stay Curious:** Maintain an insatiable curiosity about the world around you. Ask questions, seek out new experiences, and always look for opportunities to learn something new.
- **Diversify Your Learning:** Expand your horizons by learning across a broad range of subjects. Diverse knowledge not only enriches your understanding of the world but also enhances creativity and problem-solving skills.

Adapting to Change

Change is the only constant in life. The ability to adapt to change—not just to survive but to thrive—is a critical component of continuous learning. Adaptable individuals can navigate the uncertainties of life with confidence and resilience.

- **Develop Flexibility:** Practice being flexible in your

thinking and actions. Flexibility enables you to shift gears when the unexpected happens and find solutions in the face of adversity.

- **Cultivate Resilience:** Building resilience helps you bounce back from setbacks and challenges. It's about developing the emotional and mental toughness to withstand turbulence and emerge stronger.

Leonardo da Vinci

Leonardo da Vinci, the quintessential Renaissance man, embodies the principle of continuous learning and adaptation. His insatiable curiosity and relentless pursuit of knowledge across multiple disciplines—art, science, engineering, anatomy, and more—demonstrate the power of lifelong learning. Da Vinci's ability to observe the world, ask profound questions, and apply his learnings in innovative ways led to groundbreaking contributions that have stood the test of time. His legacy teaches us that the boundaries of learning and creativity are limitless when we commit to exploring, questioning, and integrating knowledge from all corners of our experience.

Elon Musk

In the modern era, Elon Musk stands as a testament to the principle of continuous learning and adaptation. Musk, known for his work with SpaceX, Tesla, and other ventures, has repeatedly ventured into fields where he initially had little to no expertise. His success across such diverse industries underscores the importance of embracing challenges, learning continuously, and applying knowledge innovatively. Musk's experience highlights that with a growth mindset and a commitment to lifelong learning, it's possible to change not just your trajectory but the world's.

As we delve deeper into the nuances of continuous learning and adaptation, remember that these principles are not just strategies for personal development but foundational elements for leading a life marked by growth, achievement, and contentment. In the following sections, we will explore practical strategies for incorporating lifelong learning into your daily routine, overcoming barriers to learning, and leveraging adaptation as a tool for personal and professional success.

Incorporating lifelong learning into your daily life requires intentionality and strategy. It's about making a conscious effort to expand your knowledge and skills, not just in areas directly related to your career or immediate interests but in a broad spectrum that enriches your understanding of the world and enhances your adaptability. Here are practical steps and methodologies to weave continuous learning and adaptation into the fabric of your everyday experience.

Building a Learning Routine

Set Learning Goals: Just as with any other area of personal development, setting specific learning goals can provide direction and focus for your educational endeavours. These goals can range from learning a new language to mastering a particular professional skill or even exploring a new hobby. The key is to align these goals with your broader aspirations and interests.

Dedicate Time for Learning: In our busy lives, finding time for additional activities can be challenging. However, dedicating even a small portion of your day to learning can have significant cumulative effects. This might mean reading articles or listening to podcasts during your commute, enrolling in online courses that you can complete at your own pace, or setting aside time each evening for reading books.

Utilize Diverse Learning Resources: The internet has democratized access to information, making it possible to learn almost anything from anywhere. Leverage online learning platforms for their wide array of courses in all fields. Additionally, books, documentaries, and even educational video channels can be excellent resources for expanding your knowledge.

Embracing Adaptability in Practice

Change, whether in our personal lives or in the broader societal and technological landscape, can often be disorienting. However, by embracing adaptability as a core principle, you can navigate these changes with grace and see them as opportunities for growth rather than obstacles.

Stay Informed: Keeping abreast of developments in your field of interest, as well as in related and completely different areas, can help you anticipate changes and adapt more quickly. Subscribe to newsletters, follow thought leaders on social media, and engage with communities of interest.

Experiment and Reflect: Adaptability is honed through practice. Don't be afraid to experiment with new approaches, technologies, or ideas. Reflect on these experiences, noting what works, and what doesn't, and how you can apply these lessons moving forward.

Cultivate a Positive Attitude Towards Failure: Adaptation often involves trial and error, and failure is an integral part of the process. View failures as learning opportunities, not as reflections of your worth or capabilities.

This mindset shift is crucial for maintaining resilience and motivation in the face of change.

Leveraging Community and Mentorship

Lifelong learning and adaptation are enriched by taking on board the perspectives and experiences of others. Engaging with a community of learners and seeking mentorship can provide support, insight, and inspiration.

Join Learning Communities: Whether online or in person, communities of like-minded learners can offer motivation, resources, and accountability. These communities can be found in professional organizations, social media groups, or local meetups.

Seek Out Mentors: A mentor who has navigated the path you're on can offer invaluable guidance, advice, and encouragement. This mentorship relationship can be formal or informal, but it should be based on mutual respect and a genuine desire for growth.

Share Your Knowledge: Teaching is a powerful learning tool. Share your knowledge and experiences with others, whether through blogging, mentoring, or speaking at community events. Teaching not only reinforces your own learning but also contributes to the growth of those around you.

Making Continuous Learning Sustainable

For lifelong learning to be sustainable, it must be integrated into the fabric of your daily life. It's about creating a lifestyle that naturally fosters growth and adaptation without feeling like a burden.

- **Integrate Learning into Daily Habits:** Incorporate

small learning activities into your existing routines. This could be as simple as listening to an educational podcast while exercising or setting aside 15 minutes before bed for reading.

- **Set Micro-Goals:** Break down your learning objectives into small, manageable goals. Celebrate achieving these micro-goals to maintain motivation and momentum.
- **Leverage Technology:** Utilize apps and digital tools to facilitate learning. Many platforms offer bite-sized lessons that fit easily into busy schedules, allowing for flexible and on-the-go learning.

Embracing Change as a Constant

In a world where change is the only constant, adaptability becomes a critical survival skill. Embracing change involves both a mindset shift and practical strategies to stay agile and responsive.

- **Anticipate Change:** Stay informed about trends and developments in your field and the world at large. Anticipating change allows you to prepare and adapt more swiftly.
- **Be Proactive, Not Reactive:** Instead of waiting for change to force your hand, actively seek out new opportunities for growth and learning. This proactive approach keeps you ahead of the curve.
- **Develop a Resilience Toolkit:** Cultivate coping strategies for dealing with uncertainty and setbacks.

This toolkit might include stress management techniques, a support network, and resources for quick learning and skill acquisition.

Fostering a Culture of Continuous Learning

For those in leadership or collaborative environments, fostering a culture of continuous learning can amplify the benefits of this principle across teams and organizations.

- **Encourage Curiosity:** Create an environment where asking questions and seeking knowledge is valued. Encourage team members to explore their interests and bring new ideas to the table.
- **Provide Learning Opportunities:** Offer access to courses, workshops, and resources that support professional and personal development. Investing in your team's growth not only enhances their skills but also their engagement and loyalty.
- **Lead by Example:** Demonstrate your commitment to continuous learning and adaptation. Share your learning experiences, successes, and failures with your team to inspire and motivate them.

The Lifelong Learner

As we wrap up this chapter on continuous learning and adaptation, it's clear that these principles are more than just pathways to personal and professional development; they are the essence of a fulfilling, dynamic life. Lifelong learning and the ability to adapt are not destinations but ongoing processes that enrich our lives, broaden our horizons, and prepare us for the future.

Continuous learning is both challenging and rewarding. It requires commitment, curiosity, and the courage to step out of your comfort zone. Yet, the rewards—new skills, deeper knowledge, enhanced adaptability, and personal growth—are immeasurable.

Remember, the principle of continuous learning and adaptation is not about constant striving or relentless change. It's about remaining open to the possibilities that life offers, embracing growth as a fundamental part of your being, and navigating the ever-changing landscape of the world with confidence and grace.

As you move forward, armed with the insights and strategies from this chapter, let the principle of continuous learning and adaptation be your guide. Let it inspire you to seek out new knowledge, to embrace change with enthusiasm, and to view every experience as an opportunity to learn, grow, and evolve.

Your journey as a lifelong learner is a testament to your commitment to living a life of purpose, passion, and perpetual growth. Embrace this new way of living with an open heart and mind, and let the adventure of continuous learning and adaptation unfold.

Chapter 5: The Principle of Positive Mental Attitude

Cultivating Light in Times of Darkness

As we travel together through "Get A Life," we've explored the foundational principles that have not only shaped my path but also illuminated the way for countless others striving for a richer, more fulfilling existence. As we venture into the heart of what I believe to be one of the most transformative principles, the power of a positive mental attitude, I invite you to join me in uncovering the profound impact positivity can have on our lives.

The Power of Positivity

My own journey towards understanding and harnessing the power of positivity wasn't born out of an inherently sunny disposition or an easy life. Like many of you, I've faced my share of dark days, challenges that seemed insurmountable, and moments of doubt that clouded my vision for the future. It was during these times that the principle of positive mental attitude became my beacon of hope.

The turning point came for me in a period of significant personal and professional struggle which I touched on earlier in this book.

As mentioned, in 2013, sitting in an apartment in Portugal, I had recently lost my successful golf and restaurant business due to an unscrupulous landlord. (That's the polite phrase I believe). Beside my ailing, expectant wife, with the weight of unpaid rent and empty cupboards pressing upon us, I encountered a moment of profound clarity and an unwavering resolve like never before. This harrowing crossroads in our lives was a place I vowed we would never revisit.

The decision, firm and irrevocable, marked a turning point—though the way forward was obscured, the commitment was as solid as steel.

At the time, the 'how' of our escape eluded me, but in retrospect, the true power lay in the act of deciding itself, a decision fueled by a potent blend of emotion and the readiness to act. This pivotal choice became a cornerstone of our journey, a testament to the transformative power of resolve underpinned by purpose and action.

It was around this time that my friend asked me to "read a book" and our world has never been the same since. I mention the word journey a lot in this book and this was the beginning of ours.

I began to immerse myself in the teachings of those who had navigated similar turbulent waters and emerged not just unscathed but stronger and more focused. What I learned was transformative: the lens through which we view our challenges significantly influences their outcome.

Cultivating a Positive Outlook

A positive mental attitude is not about denying the reality of challenges or painting over difficulties with a superficial layer of optimism. Instead, it's about choosing to focus on solutions rather than problems, and opportunities rather than obstacles. This shift in perspective doesn't happen overnight, but with intentional practice, it becomes a powerful tool for navigating life's ups and downs.

- **Practice Gratitude:** Begin each day by acknowledging

something for which you are grateful. In Portugal I started by being grateful for my loving, wonderful wife, Emma, and that she was able to get pregnant. (The doctors told her this would not be possible). The next day I added that we actually had a roof over our heads, however temporary, and I continue writing my daily gratitude to this day.

This practice sets a tone of positivity that can carry you through the day, shifting your focus from what's lacking to the abundance that exists in your life.

- **Reframe Challenges:** When faced with difficulties, ask yourself, "What can I learn from this?" or "How can this make me stronger?" Viewing challenges as opportunities for growth transforms them from roadblocks into stepping stones.
- **Surround Yourself with Positivity:** The people we surround ourselves with have a profound impact on our outlook. Seek out relationships that uplift and support you, and limit exposure to negativity, whether from individuals or media.

Overcoming Negativity

Negativity, whether internal in the form of self-doubt and criticism or external from the environment and people around us, can be a significant barrier to maintaining a positive outlook. Overcoming this negativity requires conscious effort and strategies tailored to fortify your mental and emotional resilience.

- **Mindfulness and Meditation:** These practices can help you become more aware of negative thought patterns and provide the space to choose a more positive response. Even a few minutes of meditation daily can significantly impact your ability to manage negativity.

- **Positive Affirmations:** Regularly repeating positive affirmations can reprogram your mind to focus on your strengths and goals rather than fears and doubts. Affirmations like "I am capable of overcoming any challenge that comes my way" can be powerful motivators.

- **Limit Exposure to Negativity:** Be mindful of your consumption of news and social media, and strive to engage with content that is uplifting and constructive. Similarly, seek out friendships and professional relationships that foster positivity and growth.

As I share these insights with you, it's with the deep understanding that life is fraught with challenges. Yet, it's how we choose to face these challenges that define our future. The principle of a positive mental attitude has been a guiding light in my life, illuminating the darkest of times and revealing opportunities for growth and happiness that I might otherwise have missed.

In the next segments of this chapter, we will delve deeper into practical techniques for fostering positivity in your daily life, stories of individuals who have transformed their lives through a positive outlook, and strategies for making positivity a lasting part of your personal and professional life. Together, let's explore how cultivating a positive mental attitude can not only change the way we experience the world but also how we impact it.

Transformative Stories of Positivity

Nelson Mandela: Overcoming Adversity

Nelson Mandela's life story is a profound testament to the power of a positive mental attitude in the face of seemingly insurmountable adversity. Imprisoned for 27 years for his fight against apartheid in South Africa, Mandela could have easily given in to despair and bitterness. Instead, he chose to foster a mindset of forgiveness and reconciliation, focusing on the future of his country rather than the injustices of his past. Upon his release in 1990, Mandela's unwavering commitment to peace and unity paved the way for the end of apartheid, leading to his election as South Africa's first black president in 1994. Mandela's legacy, marked by his Nobel Peace Prize in 1993 and his enduring symbol as a global advocate for human rights, exemplifies how a positive mental attitude can transform personal suffering into a force for national healing and global change.

My Wife Emma: Overcoming Ill Health

Emma, like me, was born and raised in Belfast, Northern Ireland, amidst "The Troubles." At 23, her caring spirit led her to Tanzania on a missionary expedition which lasted over seven years. This was only to be cut short by contracting malaria and the devastating news of her mother's terminal cancer diagnosis. Returning home, she devoted herself to caring for her mother and following her death, her father, all while her health was deteriorating. Diagnosed with endometriosis and chronic fatigue/M.E., Emma faced the added challenge of medications that often did more harm than good. By the time we met in 2011, she was battling profound exhaustion, yet her spirit remained unbroken.

Despite these trials, Emma's resilience has been nothing short of remarkable. Since moving to Portugal with her beloved cat, she has not only married and become a mother to three children since 2013 but has also excelled as an incredible wife, mother, and friend. Together, we continue to navigate her path toward full health, witnessing significant improvements each year, a testament to her indomitable mindset and unwavering positivity.

Elena: Spreading Positivity

Elena, a teacher by profession, recognized the power of a positive mental attitude not just in her life but in her ability to influence her students. Faced with the challenge of teaching in a low-income district where students often came to class burdened by the weight of their circumstances, Elena made it her mission to create a classroom atmosphere of hope and encouragement.

By integrating practices of positive affirmation, highlighting each student's strengths, and creating a supportive community within her classroom, Elena witnessed remarkable transformations in her students' attitudes towards learning and their futures. Her story is a testament to how positivity can extend beyond personal transformation to inspire and uplift those around us.

Conclusion: The Ripple Effect of Positivity

The stories of Nelson, Emma, and Elena are just a few examples of how a positive mental attitude can serve as a powerful catalyst for change, not only in our own lives but also in the lives of those we touch. These narratives underscore the principle that positivity is not merely a personal practice but a communal one, with the potential to create waves of change that extend far beyond our immediate sphere.

As we conclude this chapter on the Principle of Positive Mental Attitude, let these stories serve as reminders of the profound impact our outlook can have on our lives.. By choosing to embrace positivity, to learn from our challenges, and to spread light even in the face of darkness, we can transform our lives and, in doing so, inspire transformation in the world around us.

This principle, woven deeply into the fabric of our daily existence, empowers us to face the future with hope, resilience, and a deep-seated belief in the possibility of positive change.

Chapter 6: The Principle of Service and Value Creation

Beyond the Self

As we navigate through the transformative principles laid out in "Get A Life," we arrive at a juncture that, for many, marks the beginning of true fulfilment: the Principle of Service and Value Creation.

This chapter is not merely a call to action; it's an invitation to step into a broader perspective of our purpose and potential impact on the world. I've discovered, through experience, that at the heart of genuine success and satisfaction lies not in what we accumulate for ourselves but in what we contribute to others.

The Essence of Service and Value

Service and value creation are twin pillars upon which meaningful lives and careers are built. They transcend the transactional nature of everyday interactions, fostering connections that enrich both the giver and receiver. This principle is about looking beyond our immediate desires and considering how our actions, skills, and knowledge can benefit others.

- **Service as a Pathway to Growth:** Service, in its many forms, offers a powerful avenue for personal and professional growth. It challenges us to apply our talents in ways that matter, pushing us beyond our comfort zones and expanding our understanding of what we are capable of achieving.

- **Value Creation as a Measure of Success:** The value we create for others—whether through our work, our relationships, or our contributions to the community—becomes a true measure of our success. It's about making a difference, leaving a positive imprint on the world that outlasts our immediate presence.

Integrating Service and Value Creation into Daily Life

Incorporating the principle of service and value creation into our lives requires a shift in perspective and, often, in priorities. It's about identifying opportunities to serve and create value in every aspect of our lives.

- **Start Small:** Service and value creation don't have to involve grand gestures. Small acts of kindness, offering your skills to help someone in need, or contributing to community projects can have a profound impact.
- **Leverage Your Unique Talents:** Each of us has a unique set of skills and talents. Identifying how these can be used to serve others not only amplifies our impact but also brings a deeper sense of fulfilment and purpose to our work.

Examples of Service and Value Creation

Throughout my career, I've encountered countless individuals whose commitment to service and value creation has not only transformed the lives of others but has also brought them immeasurable satisfaction and success.

- **The Story of Clara:** Clara, a software developer, used her skills to create educational apps for children with learning disabilities. Her work, driven by a desire to serve, has touched the lives of thousands of children and families, providing them with resources that were previously inaccessible.
- **Community Gardens:** In another example, a group of neighbours transformed a vacant piece of ground into a community garden. This project not only beautified the neighbourhood but also provided a source of fresh food and a gathering place for the community, creating value that extended far beyond the initial investment of time and effort.
- **Writing This Book:** The decision to pen this book sprang from a deep-seated desire to extend a helping hand, to impart value not only to those within my immediate circle but also to individuals far beyond my reach. The insights and lessons that have profoundly shaped my life in recent years hold the potential to transform lives. This belief instils in me a sense of duty to share the wealth of knowledge I've amassed.

Writing this book has become a journey of growth and contribution and an immense source of fulfilment for me. It has reinforced my belief in the power of sharing one's experience to enlighten the paths of others.

- **Strategies for Cultivating a Service-Oriented Mindset**

Developing a mindset that prioritizes service and value creation involves intentional practice and reflection. Here are some strategies to help cultivate this perspective:

- **Reflect on Your Impact:** Regularly take time to reflect on the impact your actions have on others. Ask yourself how you can use your position, skills, or resources to serve more effectively.
- **Seek Out Needs:** Be proactive in looking for needs within your community or industry that align with your abilities to contribute. This active approach to service can reveal opportunities you may not have previously considered.
- **Embrace Empathy:** Cultivating empathy is crucial for service and value creation. It allows us to understand the needs and experiences of others, guiding our efforts in more meaningful and impactful directions.

Expanding the Circle of Impact

As we venture deeper into the practice of service and value creation, it becomes clear that the potential for impact extends far beyond individual interactions. By cultivating a mindset focused on contributing positively to the world, we can initiate a ripple effect, inspiring others to act similarly and thereby expanding the circle of impact.

Collaboration and Partnership: One of the most powerful ways to amplify service and value creation is through collaboration. Whether it's partnering with local organizations, joining forces with colleagues, or engaging in community projects, working together magnifies our ability to make a difference. For instance, a collaboration between businesses and non-profits can lead to initiatives that address community needs more effectively than either could alone.

Educating and Inspiring Others: Sharing your journey of service and value creation can inspire and educate others. By documenting your experiences, challenges, and successes, you provide a roadmap for others interested in making a positive impact. Workshops, mentorship programs, and speaking engagements are platforms where these stories can be shared, encouraging a culture of service and contribution.

The Role of Mentorship in Service

Mentorship stands out as a profound example of service and value creation, embodying the essence of these principles through the act of guiding and supporting others.

My recent history, for instance, has been significantly shaped by mentors who generously shared their wisdom, challenges, and insights, helping me navigate my path more effectively.

Becoming a Mentor: Stepping into a mentorship role allows you to pass on valuable lessons and insights, offering guidance that can help others avoid pitfalls and seize opportunities more confidently. It's a role that benefits the mentor as well, offering a sense of fulfilment and the opportunity to reflect on and solidify one's own knowledge and experiences.

Seeking Out Mentors: Actively seeking mentorship can accelerate your growth and understanding of service and value creation. Look for individuals whose lives and careers embody these principles, and don't hesitate to reach out. Most people are willing to share their knowledge and experiences, espccially if they see a genuine desire to learn and grow.

Mentorship: Seeking professional development, I pursued training as a Professional Coach and achieved certification as a Living the Legacy Mentor, under the tutelage of Bob Proctor, alongside qualifying as a certified Belief-clearing Practitioner and Professional Life Coach.

These accomplishments have laid a solid foundation for me, empowering me to step into the role of an effective mentor. Continuous learning and certification have not only enriched my knowledge base but have also finely honed my ability to guide others on their journeys toward personal and professional fulfilment.

Sustainable Service: Balancing Giving and Self-Care

While the drive to serve and create value is commendable, it's important to balance these efforts with self-care. Sustainable service means recognizing our limits and ensuring we don't deplete our own resources. This balance is crucial for maintaining the energy and enthusiasm needed to continue making a positive impact over the long term.

Setting Boundaries: It's essential to set healthy boundaries around your service efforts. This might mean learning to say no, delegating responsibilities, or taking breaks when needed. Remember, you can't pour from an empty cup; taking care of yourself enables you to serve others more effectively.

Self-Care Practices: Incorporate self-care practices into your routine to recharge and maintain your well-being. This can include physical activities, hobbies, meditation, or spending time with loved ones. Self-care is not selfish; it's a vital component of a sustainable approach to service and value creation.

The Joy of Giving: Personal Fulfillment Through Service

The joy and fulfillment derived from serving others and creating value are unparalleled. This principle has been a guiding light in my life, offering clarity during times of uncertainty and a sense of purpose that transcends personal achievements. The act of giving, without expectation of return, aligns us with a higher purpose and connects us to the broader tapestry of human experience.

In embracing the Principle of Service and Value Creation, we want to enrich our lives and the lives of those around us. It leads to deeper connections, a stronger sense of community, and the realization that our greatest successes are measured by the positive impact we have on the world.

As we conclude this segment, reflect on how you can integrate service and value creation into your life more deeply. Consider the skills, resources, and passions you possess that can benefit others, and take steps to engage in acts of service that resonate with your values and goals. In doing so, you'll discover that the true essence of fulfilment lies not in what we acquire for ourselves but in what we contribute to the lives of others

As we bring our focus on the Principle of Service and Value Creation to a close, it's essential to consider the broader implications of embedding these ideals into our lives.

Integrating service and value creation extends beyond individual acts of kindness or professional achievements; it's about cultivating a lifestyle that inherently values and promotes the well-being of others alongside our own.

Building a Legacy of Service

One of the most profound aspects of deeply committing to service and value creation is the legacy it establishes. A legacy of service transcends material success, embedding your influence in the lives you've touched and the positive changes you've contributed to the world. It's about leaving behind a trail of inspiration, a blueprint for others to follow, and a foundation upon which future generations can build.

- **Document Your Journey:** Sharing your story, the challenges you've faced, the lessons you've learned, and the impact you've made, can be incredibly powerful. Whether through writing, speaking, or mentoring, your experiences can light the way for others and amplify the reach of your service.

- **Engage in Sustainable Practices:** Ensure that your efforts in service and value creation are sustainable and ethical. This involves considering the long-term impacts of your actions and striving to create solutions that are beneficial for all stakeholders. Sustainable service is about creating positive change that endures and respects the resources and communities involved.

The Ripple Effect of Positivity and Service

The beauty of service and value creation is not just in the immediate impact but in the ripple effect it generates. Acts of service and efforts to create value often inspire others to do the same, setting off a chain reaction of positivity and impact. This ripple effect can transform communities, industries, and even societies, creating waves of change that reach far beyond the initial act.

- **Celebrate and Support Others' Efforts:** Recognizing and supporting the service and value creation efforts of others not only amplifies their impact but also fosters a culture of generosity and collaboration. Celebrate the successes and contributions of your peers, and look for ways to support and elevate their work.
- **Cultivate a Community of Service:** Engage with or build communities that prioritize service and value creation. These communities can become powerful incubators for innovative solutions to social challenges, providing a support network for individuals committed to making a difference.

The Personal Rewards of a Service-Oriented Life

While the primary motivation behind service and value creation should not be personal gain, the truth is that these principles bring immense personal rewards. From the deep satisfaction and fulfilment that come from making a meaningful difference to the growth and learning opportunities that service presents, the benefits to the individual are significant.

- **Enhanced Personal Growth:** Engaging in service challenges you to grow in empath
- y, leadership, and problem-solving skills. It provides opportunities for personal reflection and development that are unique to the experience of giving.
- **Increased Sense of Purpose:** Living a life oriented towards service and value creation offers a profound sense of purpose and direction. It aligns your daily actions with your values and aspirations, providing a clear sense of why you do what you do.

Conclusion: A Call to Action

As we conclude this exploration of the Principle of Service and Value Creation, I extend to you a call to action. Consider how you can incorporate these principles into your life more fully. Reflect on the talents, resources, and passions you possess and how they can be utilized to serve others and create value in the world around you.

Embracing service and value creation offers endless possibilities for impact and fulfilment. It's a road that I have walked and continue to walk, finding along the way that the greatest successes are those that benefit not just ourselves but the broader community and world we are part of.

Let this chapter not just be a reading exercise but a spark that ignites a deeper commitment to living a life marked by service and value creation. Together, let's transform our lives and the world around us through the power of positive impact.

Chapter 7: The Principle of Health and Well-being

A Harmonious Balance

So far, through "Get A Life," we've explored various principles essential for personal and professional fulfilment. Now, we delve into a principle that forms the bedrock of our ability to pursue and enjoy these achievements: the Principle of Health and Well-being. This chapter isn't just about maintaining physical health; it's about recognizing the intricate dance between physical fitness, mental wellness, and productivity that enables us to lead truly enriched lives.

As someone deeply committed to not only cultivating a rich, fulfilling life but also sharing the roadmap with others, I've found that balancing these aspects of health and well-being is crucial. My personal routine, which includes intermittent fasting, regular gym sessions, playing soccer, listening to mentors, and daily reflections of gratitude, is a testament to the holistic approach to health and well-being I advocate.

The Pillars of Physical Health

Physical health is the foundation upon which our mental and emotional well-being rests. Without it, our ability to pursue goals, overcome challenges, and enjoy life's pleasures is significantly compromised.

- **Intermittent Fasting:** Eating Intermittently, for me this is trying to eat within an eight hour window each day, has taught me the importance of not just what we eat but when we eat. This practice has not only helped in managing weight but also in improving focus and energy levels, demonstrating how tweaking our eating patterns can have profound effects on our health.

- **Regular Exercise:** The benefits of regular physical activity extend far beyond the physical. While I go to the gym several times a week and play soccer 2 or 3 times a week to maintain physical fitness, these activities also serve as an outlet for stress, a source of joy, and a tool for building discipline and resilience. For a group of middle-aged Dads, it's also great therapy to go kick a ball for an hour and have a chat.

Cultivating Mental Wellness

Mental wellness is equally vital, influencing our perceptions, decisions, and interactions with the world. It encompasses our emotional, psychological, and social well-being.

- **Listening to Mentors:** Incorporating wisdom from mentors into my daily routine has been instrumental in maintaining mental wellness. It provides perspective, inspires growth, and fosters a mindset geared towards continuous learning and positivity.
- **Gratitude Practice:** My daily gratitude practice, where I reflect on and jot down the aspects of my life I'm grateful for, has profoundly impacted my mental health. This simple act shifts focus from what's lacking to the abundance present in our lives,

fostering a sense of contentment and well-being. I start with "I am so happy and grateful now that..." And bring the future into the present.

Balancing Productivity

In today's fast-paced world, productivity is often equated with success. However, true productivity cannot be sustained without a solid foundation of physical and mental health.

- **Setting Realistic Goals:** Overcommitment can lead to stress and burnout. Setting realistic goals, informed by an understanding of our physical and mental capacities, ensures that our drive for productivity doesn't come at the expense of our well-being.
- **Incorporating Breaks:** Regular breaks are not a sign of weakness but a necessary component of sustained productivity. They provide moments of rest for the body and mind, allowing us to return to our tasks with renewed energy and focus.

Practical Health and Wellness Tips

Incorporating health and well-being into daily life can seem daunting, but it doesn't have to be. Here are some practical tips inspired by my routine and supported by health experts:

- **Start Small:** Incorporate small, manageable changes into your routine. This could mean starting with a shorter fasting window, committing to physical activity once a week, or writing down one thing you're grateful for each day.

- **Find Activities You Enjoy:** The best form of exercise is the one you enjoy and can stick with. Whether it's soccer, yoga, swimming, or dancing, choosing activities that bring joy can make maintaining physical health a pleasure rather than a chore.
- **Seek Support:** Achieving health and wellness can be more enjoyable and sustainable with support. Whether it's a workout buddy, a mentor, or a community of like-minded individuals, having support can provide motivation and accountability.

As we navigate the principles of health and well-being, remember that getting there is highly personal and ever-evolving. What works for one person may not work for another, and that's okay. The key is to listen to your body, honour your mental and emotional needs, and adjust your routine as necessary to maintain balance and harmony in your life.

Achieving your health and wellness goal requires more than just a set routine; it demands an understanding of the dynamic interplay between our habits and our overall quality of life. This deeper exploration into the Principle of Health and Well-being focuses on enhancing our approach to physical activity, nutrition, and mental health, and integrating these elements into a cohesive lifestyle that promotes sustained well-being.

Enhancing Physical Activity

While my routine includes regular gym sessions and soccer, the essence of maintaining physical health extends beyond structured exercise. It's about infusing movement into your daily life in ways that feel natural and enjoyable. Here are additional strategies to consider:

- **Variety in Exercise:** To prevent boredom and plateauing, introduce variety into your exercise regimen. This could mean trying new sports, varying your workout routines, or incorporating outdoor activities like hiking or cycling. The goal is to keep your body guessing and your mind engaged.
- **Listen to Your Body:** Paying attention to your body's signals is crucial. While consistency is key to seeing results, understanding when to push through and when to rest is equally important. This balance prevents injury and ensures that exercise remains a source of joy rather than a chore.

Mindful Nutrition

Intermittent fasting has been a significant part of my health routine, but mindful nutrition encompasses more than timing your meals. It involves being conscious of what you eat and how it affects your body and mind.

- **Whole Foods Over Processed:** Aim to base your diet around whole foods. Fruits, vegetables, lean proteins, whole grains, and healthy fats should make up the bulk of your diet. These foods provide the nutrients your body needs to function optimally and support mental health.

- **Hydration:** Often overlooked, proper hydration is critical for physical health and cognitive function. Water supports digestion, nutrient absorption, and muscle recovery, and even mild dehydration can impact mood and energy levels.

Prioritizing Mental Health

Listening to mentors daily and maintaining a gratitude book are practices that significantly contribute to my mental wellness. Expanding on these, consider the following strategies to nurture your mental health:

- **Digital Detoxes:** Regularly unplugging from digital devices can reduce stress and improve sleep quality. Set aside time each day or week when you disconnect from screens, allowing your mind to rest and recharge.
- **Mindfulness Practices:** Beyond meditation, mindfulness can be practised in everyday activities like eating, walking, or listening to music. The key is to be fully present and engaged in the moment, which can reduce stress and enhance your sense of well-being.

Integration for Sustained Well-being

Balancing physical health, mental wellness, and productivity doesn't mean equal parts of each every day. It's about finding a rhythm that suits your life and allows you to thrive. Integration means recognizing when your body needs rest, when your mind seeks stimulation, and how to align your productivity goals with your health needs.

- **Adaptability:** Your health and wellness routine should be adaptable. Life throws curveballs, and your ability to adjust your routine in response to changing circumstances is crucial for long-term success. This might mean shortening your workout on busy days or choosing restorative yoga over high-intensity training when you're feeling stressed.

- **Holistic Health Tools:** Consider using apps or journals to track your progress and reflect on how different aspects of your health routine affect your overall well-being. This can help you identify patterns and make informed adjustments to your routine.

- **Community and Connection:** Engage with communities that share your health and wellness goals. This could be a local sports team, a meditation group, or an online forum. Sharing experiences and challenges with others can provide support, motivation, and a sense of belonging.

Incorporating the Principle of Health and Well-being into your life is an ongoing process of learning, experimenting, and growing. It's about crafting a lifestyle that honours your physical, mental, and emotional needs, enabling you to pursue your goals with vigour and resilience. My experiences have taught me that health is the true wealth, and well-being is the foundation upon which fulfilling lives are built. By adopting practices that nurture your body and mind, you set the stage for a life rich in experiences, achievements, and joy.

As we draw this chapter to a close, it's important to reflect on the profound truth that health and well-being are not merely aspects of our lives; they are the very essence of our ability to live fully and meaningfully. This principle has never been more poignant for me than in witnessing my wife's long battle with chronic fatigue.

Living with Chronic Illness: A Personal Reflection

For over 15 years, my wife has faced the daily challenges posed by chronic fatigue syndrome. It's a condition that has tested our resilience, our understanding of health, and the depth of our commitment to finding balance and well-being amidst adversity. Her experience underscores the critical importance of health—not just as a personal responsibility but as a treasure.

The Single Wish of Health: The saying "a *well* person has many wishes, but a sick person has one" resonates deeply within our household. It serves as a constant reminder of the fundamental value of health and the profound impact illness can have on one's life, aspirations, and the simple ability to engage with the world.

Strategies for Supporting Loved Ones

Living with or supporting someone with a chronic illness can profoundly affect your perspective on health and well-being. Here are some strategies that have been instrumental for us:

- **Empathy and Understanding:** Cultivating a deep sense of empathy and striving to understand the lived experience of your loved one is crucial. It's about listening, truly listening, to their needs, fears, and hopes.

- **Seeking Balance:** Finding a balance between caregiving and self-care can be challenging but is essential. Neglecting your own well-being can compromise your ability to provide support and maintain the resilience needed over the long haul.
- **Advocacy and Research:** Becoming an advocate for your loved one and actively engaging in research about their condition can open doors to new treatments and understanding. It's a journey we've embarked on together, seeking not just answers but also hope.

Integrating Wellness into Every Aspect of Life

This shared experience has also reinforced the importance of integrating the principle of health and well-being into every aspect of our lives. It's about more than just physical fitness or mental health in isolation; it's about nurturing a holistic sense of wellness that encompasses emotional, social, and spiritual dimensions.

- **Holistic Approaches to Health:** Exploring holistic approaches to health, including diet, exercise, mindfulness, and alternative therapies, can offer new avenues for managing chronic conditions and enhancing overall well-being.
- **The Role of Community:** The support of a

compassionate community, whether found in support groups, online forums, or among friends and family, can be a source of strength and comfort. These communities offer not just practical advice but also a sense of belonging and understanding.

A Commitment to Well-being

In sharing this part of my journey, I hope to illuminate the inextricable link between health and the richness of life. The challenges we've faced have brought into sharp focus the reality that health is the foundation upon which all else is built. It has taught us to cherish each moment of wellness, to approach health as a holistic endeavour encompassing mind, body, and spirit, and to never take for granted the blessings of good health.

As you, the reader, move forward, let this chapter serve as both a guide and a reminder. A guide to cultivating health and well-being through mindful practices, balanced living, and a commitment to growth. And a reminder of the preciousness of health, as articulated in the poignant truth that while the well may have many wishes, the one wish of the sick is to find health once more.

In embracing the Principle of Health and Well-being, we not only enhance our own lives but also extend our capacity to support and uplift those around us. Let us commit to this principle with compassion, mindfulness, and an unwavering dedication to nurturing the well-being of ourselves and our loved ones.

Chapter 8: The Principle of Time Management and Productivity

So far, we've explored various principles essential for cultivating a rich, fulfilling existence. As we delve into the Principle of Time Management and Productivity, we uncover the strategies that not only maximize our efficiency but also ensure our actions align with our deepest values and aspirations. Drawing from a wealth of wisdom found in the teachings on success and personal development, this chapter synthesizes the best strategies into a personal system that has significantly enhanced my own productivity and time management.

Understanding the Value of Time

Time, unlike other resources, is irreplaceable. Once spent, it cannot be regained, making its effective management crucial for achieving our goals and living a life of purpose. Recognizing time's intrinsic value is the first step towards managing it wisely. This realization compels us to make conscious choices about how we allocate our hours, focusing on activities that align with our goals and bring us fulfilment.

Prioritization: The Key to Effective Time Management

The essence of effective time management lies in prioritization. By distinguishing between what is urgent and what is important, we can ensure that our time is spent on activities that truly matter. This involves:

- **Creating a Priority List:** Each day, identify the tasks that are most critical to your goals and well-being. These should take precedence in your schedule.

- **Understanding the Pareto Principle:** Often referred to as the 80/20 rule, this principle suggests that 80% of outcomes result from 20% of all efforts. Focus on the tasks that yield the most significant results.

Time Blocking: A Personal System for Productivity

One of the most effective strategies I've incorporated into my life is time blocking. This technique involves dedicating specific blocks of time to different tasks or activities. By allocating a set period to focus on a single task, I minimize distractions and increase my efficiency. Here's how you can implement time blocking:

- **Plan Your Day:** At the beginning of each day or the night before, divide your day into blocks of time, assigning each block a specific task or activity.
- **Include Breaks:** Ensure that you include short breaks between time blocks to rest and recharge. These breaks are crucial for maintaining high levels of productivity throughout the day.

The Two-Minute Rule

A simple yet powerful tool for overcoming procrastination and managing smaller tasks is the Two-Minute Rule. If a task can be done in two minutes or less, do it immediately. This rule helps keep your task list manageable and prevents the accumulation of minor tasks that can later become overwhelming.

Eliminating Distractions

In an age where distractions are constantly vying for our attention, creating an environment conducive to focus is essential. This includes:

- **Digital Detox:** Allocate specific times of the day to check emails and social media. Outside of these times, keep your devices on silent or in another room.
- **Focused Environment:** Tailor your workspace to minimize distractions. This might mean using noise-cancelling headphones, decluttering your desk, or using apps that block distracting websites.

The Power of Reflection

An often overlooked aspect of time management and productivity is the power of reflection. Regularly reviewing how you spend your time can provide valuable insights into your productivity patterns and help you make adjustments as needed. This reflection can be done through:

- **Weekly Reviews:** Dedicate time each week to review your accomplishments, assess the effectiveness of your time management strategies, and plan for the week ahead.
- **Adjusting Strategies:** Based on your reflections, be willing to adjust your strategies. What works well one week may not be as effective the next, so flexibility is key.

Incorporating these time management and productivity strategies has profoundly impacted my ability to achieve my goals while maintaining a sense of balance in my life. By understanding the value of time, prioritizing effectively, minimizing distractions, and regularly reflecting on our practices, we can ensure that our most precious resource is spent on what truly matters.

Building upon the foundation of effective time management and productivity strategies, let's delve deeper into advanced techniques and personal systems that further enhance our ability to navigate our days with intention and efficiency.

The Art of Delegation

One of the most significant shifts in my approach to time management was embracing the art of delegation. Recognizing that trying to do everything oneself is neither practical nor efficient was a game-changer. Delegation not only frees up your time for tasks that require your unique skills and attention but also empowers others by trusting them with responsibilities.

- **Identify Delegable Tasks:** Start by identifying tasks that do not require your specific expertise. These could range from administrative duties to certain aspects of project management.
- **Choose the Right People:** Delegate tasks to individuals whose skills and goals align with the work. Providing clear instructions and the necessary resources is crucial for their success and your peace of mind.

Mastering the Eisenhower Matrix

The Eisenhower Matrix has been a cornerstone of my time management system, helping me distinguish between tasks based on their urgency and importance. This matrix divides tasks into four quadrants:

- **Important and Urgent:** Tasks that require immediate attention and are directly related to your goals.
- **Important but Not Urgent:** Tasks that are crucial to your long-term success but do not need to be completed immediately.
- **Urgent but Not Important:** Tasks that demand your attention but do not contribute significantly to your goals.
- **Not Urgent and Not Important:** Low-priority tasks that offer little to no value.

By categorizing tasks in this manner, you can focus your energy on what truly moves the needle forward, ensuring that your time is spent on activities that align with your goals and values.

Leveraging Technology for Productivity

In an era where technology can be both a distraction and a tool, learning to leverage it effectively has been key to enhancing my productivity. Apps and software that streamline workflows, automate repetitive tasks, and facilitate communication have become integral to my daily routine.

- **Task Management Tools:** Utilizing apps like Trello, Asana, or Todoist can help keep your projects and tasks organized, providing a visual overview of your priorities and deadlines.

- **Automation Tools:** Tools like Zapier can automate repetitive tasks, from scheduling social media posts to managing email alerts, saving you time for more strategic activities.

Prioritizing Self-Care in Time Management

An often overlooked aspect of time management is the integration of self-care into our schedules. I've learned that neglecting self-care in the pursuit of productivity is counterproductive. Incorporating activities that rejuvenate your mind, body, and spirit is essential for sustaining long-term productivity.

- **Schedule Downtime:** Just as you would schedule a meeting or a work session, schedule time for activities that relax and recharge you. This could be anything from reading and hobbies to exercise and meditation.
- **Listen to Your Body:** Pay attention to your body's cues. If you're feeling fatigued or stressed, it might be more productive to take a break and return to your tasks with renewed energy.

Continuous Improvement through Reflection

Adopting a mindset of continuous improvement has been critical in refining my time management and productivity practices. Regular reflection allows me to assess what's working, identify areas for improvement, and adapt my strategies to meet evolving challenges and goals.

- **End-of-Day Review:** Spend a few minutes at the end of each day reviewing what you accomplished, what challenges you faced, and how you can improve your approach moving forward.
- **Experiment with New Techniques:** Be open to experimenting with new time management and productivity strategies. What works for others may not work for you, and vice versa. The key is to find a system that resonates with your work style and life goals.

Incorporating these advanced time management and productivity strategies has not only improved my ability to achieve my goals but also enhanced my overall well-being. By delegating effectively, utilizing the Eisenhower Matrix, leveraging technology, prioritizing self-care, and committing to continuous improvement, I've been able to create a more balanced, fulfilling life.

As we conclude our exploration into the Principle of Time Management and Productivity, it becomes clear that effectively managing our time is not just about squeezing more tasks into our day. It's about making intentional choices that align our daily actions with our deepest values and long-term objectives. Through the integration of prioritization, delegation, strategic use of technology, and a commitment to self-care and continuous improvement, we can transform our approach to time and productivity, leading to a more balanced and fulfilling life.

Implementing Time Management Strategies: Practical Steps

To transition from understanding to action, here are practical steps to start implementing the time management and productivity strategies discussed in this chapter:

1. **Conduct a Time Audit:** Spend a week tracking how you spend your time. Identify activities that consume your time but don't contribute to your goals. This insight is crucial for making informed adjustments to your routine.

2. **Set Clear, Achievable Goals:** Define what you want to accomplish in the short and long term. Use these goals to guide your prioritization and decision-making processes, ensuring that your efforts are aligned with your objectives.

3. **Implement the Eisenhower Matrix:** Start categorizing your tasks based on urgency and importance. Focus on completing tasks that are both important and urgent, and schedule time for important but not urgent activities. Learn to delegate or eliminate tasks that do not significantly contribute to your goals.

4. **Begin Time Blocking:** Allocate specific blocks of time for different activities or tasks in your calendar. Be sure to include blocks for breaks and personal time. This method helps ensure that you dedicate focused attention to your priorities while maintaining a balanced schedule.

5. **Embrace Delegation:** Identify tasks that can be delegated to others. Start small if you're not used to delegating, and gradually increase as you become

more comfortable with the process. Remember, delegation is not about offloading work; it's about empowering others and focusing on your strengths.

6. **Leverage Technology Wisely:** Explore apps and tools designed to enhance productivity and streamline workflows. Start with one or two tools that address your most pressing needs, whether it's task management, scheduling, or automating repetitive tasks.

7. **Schedule Self-Care:** Make self-care a non-negotiable part of your schedule. Whether it's exercise, hobbies, or simply downtime, ensuring that you recharge is vital for sustaining productivity and well-being.

8. **Reflect and Adjust Regularly:** Set aside time weekly or monthly to review your progress, challenges, and the effectiveness of your time management strategies. Be prepared to make adjustments based on what you learn about your habits, preferences, and changing circumstances.

Moving Forward with Intention

As we wrap up this chapter, I encourage you to approach time management and productivity not as a rigid set of rules to follow but as a flexible framework to live by. The strategies and insights shared here are meant to serve as a starting point, a foundation upon which you can build a system that works uniquely for you.

Remember, the ultimate goal of managing our time effectively is to create a life that is not only productive but also meaningful and fulfilling. It's about carving out space for the things that matter most, pursuing our passions with vigour, and making room for growth, discovery, and joy.

Incorporating these time management and productivity principles into your life may require patience and practice, but the rewards—increased clarity, achievement, and balance—are well worth the effort. Keep in mind that time is a finite resource, but with intentional management, its potential to enrich our lives is limitless.

Final Thoughts

Let this chapter be a catalyst for change in your approach to time and productivity. Begin by implementing one or two strategies that resonate with you, and gradually incorporate more as you find what works best. Along the way, celebrate your successes, learn from your challenges, and remain open to evolving your strategies as you grow.

Through intentional time management and productivity practices, we can transform not just how we work, but how we live—crafting a life that reflects our values, fulfills our potential, and brings us true joy and satisfaction.

Chapter 9: The Principle of Resilience and Adaptability

Forged in Adversity

As we turn the page to the next chapter of "Get a Life," we delve into principles deeply personal to me—Resilience and Adaptability. These are not just abstract concepts but lived experiences, shaped by years of navigating the challenges life has thrown my way. From growing up in Strabane during the Northern Ireland "troubles" to overcoming bullying in secondary school and facing financial ruin in 2013, my journey has been a testament to the power of resilience and the ability to adapt in the face of adversity.

Roots of Resilience: Growing Up in Strabane

Growing up in Strabane during the "troubles" in Northern Ireland presented a backdrop of conflict and uncertainty. Yet, it was within this environment that the seeds of resilience were sown. The community's strength, unity, and unwavering spirit in the face of external turmoil taught me valuable lessons about the power of resilience. It showed me that even in the darkest times, hope and perseverance can guide us through.

Overcoming Bullying: A Lesson in Personal Strength

Secondary school brought its own set of challenges, notably bullying. These experiences, while painful, taught me crucial lessons about self-worth and the inner strength required to rise above negativity. It was a period of intense personal growth, where I learned to assert my value and discovered the resilience within me to overcome personal attacks on my character and well-being.

Financial Adversity: Turning the Tide in 2013

Perhaps one of the most transformative periods of my life was in 2013, when I found myself facing financial ruin. The experience of being broke was not just a financial crisis but a profound test of my resilience and adaptability. It forced me to re-evaluate my path, make difficult decisions, and ultimately, pivot towards new opportunities. This period of adversity became a turning point, leading to growth and success I hadn't previously imagined possible.

Real-Life Examples of Resistance and Adaptability

My story is but one among countless tales of resilience and adaptability. Across the globe, individuals face and overcome adversity in myriad forms, drawing on inner strength and the support of those around them.

Malala Yousafzai's Fight for Education

Malala Yousafzai's story is a powerful testament to resilience. After surviving an assassination attempt by the Taliban for advocating girls' education in Pakistan, she didn't retreat in fear. Instead, she emerged even stronger, becoming a global symbol of the fight for education rights. This underscores that resilience is not just about surviving; it's about thriving and fighting for what you believe in, even in the face of life-threatening adversity.

Developing Resilience: Guidance and Strategies

Drawing from these experiences, both personal and observed, here are strategies to cultivate resilience and adaptability:

- **Embrace Challenges as Opportunities:** View each challenge as an opportunity for growth. Ask yourself what lessons can be learned and how these experiences can strengthen you.

- **Build a Support Network:** Surround yourself with people who uplift and support you. The strength we draw from others is invaluable during times of adversity.
- **Maintain Perspective:** Keep challenges in perspective. Remember that adversity is often temporary, and with perseverance, you can emerge stronger on the other side.
- **Cultivate a Positive Mindset:** A positive outlook can significantly impact your ability to bounce back from setbacks. Practice gratitude and focus on the positives in your life, even during tough times.
- **Stay Flexible:** Adaptability is key to resilience. Be open to changing course and exploring new routes when faced with roadblocks.

As we navigate the complexities of life, the principles of resilience and adaptability are our most trusted allies. They enable us to face adversity with courage, to learn from our experiences, and to continually grow and evolve. My life, marked by periods of conflict, bullying, and financial hardship, along with the inspiring stories of individuals like Malala Yousafzai and earlier,Nelson Mandela, serves as a reminder that our greatest trials often lead to our most profound triumphs.

Building on the foundation of resilience and adaptability, we delve deeper into the mechanics of these vital life skills, exploring how they can be cultivated and strengthened through intentional practice and mindset shifts. Resilience is not about avoiding adversity but learning to navigate it with grace, learning from each experience, and emerging stronger and more adaptable.

Nurturing Resilience Through Self-Care

An often overlooked aspect of building resilience is the role of self-care. In the throes of adversity, taking care of our physical, emotional, and mental well-being becomes even more crucial. It's about creating a strong foundation from which to face challenges, ensuring we have the energy, clarity, and strength to persevere.

- **Prioritize Physical Health:** Regular exercise, adequate sleep, and nutritious eating habits are not just good for the body; they're essential for mental resilience. My routine of intermittent fasting, gym sessions, and playing soccer not only keeps me physically fit but also mentally sharp and emotionally balanced.

- **Cultivate Emotional Resilience:** Practices such as mindfulness meditation, journaling, and engaging in hobbies that bring joy can significantly bolster emotional resilience. These activities provide a necessary outlet for stress, allowing for emotional processing and renewal.

- **Mental Fortitude:** Engaging with inspirational content, whether through reading, podcasts, or conversations with mentors, can reinforce a resilient mindset. It's about filling your mental reservoir with affirmations of strength, adaptability, and perseverance.

The Role of Community in Building Resilience

No one is an island and adversity is often lightened by the support and understanding of a community. Building a network of support, whether through friends, family, or support groups, provides a safety net that can catch us when we fall and propel us forward.

- **Seek Support:** Don't hesitate to reach out for help when needed. Sharing your struggles can lighten the load and provide new perspectives on overcoming challenges.
- **Offer Support:** Similarly, be there for others in their times of need. Offering support not only helps others but can also reinforce your own sense of purpose and resilience.

Adaptability in Action

Adaptability is the companion of resilience, allowing us to pivot in response to changing circumstances and emerge stronger from the experience. It involves a willingness to let go of old ways that no longer serve us and embrace new approaches with openness and curiosity.

- **Stay Open to Learning:** View every challenge as a learning opportunity. Staying curious and open-minded helps in adapting to new situations more fluidly.

- **Flexibility in Planning:** While having goals and plans is important, maintaining flexibility allows you to adjust as circumstances change. It's about having a clear direction but being open to different ways to reach your destination.

Real-Life Application: Turning Adversity into Advantage

My experience of financial hardship is a prime example of adaptability in action. Faced with what seemed like insurmountable obstacles, I had to reassess my path, make difficult decisions, and adapt to new realities. This period of adversity was not only a test of resilience but also an opportunity to move towards new opportunities that aligned more closely with my values and goals. It was through this process of adaptation that I discovered new avenues for growth and success.

Inspirational Stories of Resilience and Adaptability

Beyond my story, history and the world today are filled with examples of individuals who have turned adversity into advantage, demonstrating remarkable resilience and adaptability.

- **A Local Business Pivot:** A local cafe, faced with closure during the global pandemic, exemplified adaptability by shifting to online orders and delivery and transforming part of its space into a small grocery. This pivot not only kept the business afloat but also deepened its connection with the community.

- **Personal Triumph Over Illness:** A friend, battling a chronic illness, used her period of recovery to write a book about her experience, turning her struggle into a source of inspiration and support for others facing similar challenges.

These stories underscore that resilience and adaptability are not just responses to adversity but powerful catalysts for transformation and growth.

Continuous Growth Through Resilience and Adaptability

Resilience and adaptability are not just tools for surviving; they are essential for thriving. They enable us to navigate the ebb and flow of experiences with grace and to turn potential setbacks into opportunities for growth and development.

Developing a Resilient Mindset

A resilient mindset is cultivated through intentional practice and reflection. It involves a commitment to viewing life's challenges as catalysts for growth, rather than insurmountable obstacles.

- **Practice Positive Reframing:** When faced with adversity, consciously shift your perspective to focus on potential positive outcomes or lessons. This doesn't mean ignoring the difficulty of situations but choosing to see them through a lens of growth.
- **Embrace Failure as Feedback:** Each failure provides invaluable feedback. Instead of viewing it as a negative endpoint, see it as part of the process of learning and growing. This mindset encourages

resilience by framing setbacks as necessary steps toward success.

- **Commit to Lifelong Learning:** Resilience is bolstered by a commitment to continuous personal and professional development. By always being in a state of learning, you equip yourself with new skills and knowledge that enhance your ability to adapt.

Strategies for Enhancing Adaptability

Adaptability requires a proactive approach to life's uncertainties. It's about anticipating change, being prepared to adjust your plans, and finding innovative solutions to new problems.

- **Stay Informed:** Keeping abreast of trends and changes in your field and the world at large can help you anticipate shifts and adapt more quickly.
- **Build a Diverse Skill Set:** Cultivate a broad range of skills that can be applied in various contexts. This diversity enhances your ability to pivot and adapt when one road is blocked.
- **Foster an Agile Environment:** Whether in personal projects or professional settings, create an environment that encourages experimentation and flexibility. An agile approach allows for rapid adaptation to change and fosters a culture of resilience.

Embedding Resilience and Adaptability in Daily Life

Integrating resilience and adaptability into our daily lives means making conscious choices that reflect these values. It's about creating habits and routines that reinforce our ability to bounce back and pivot when necessary.

- **Daily Reflection:** Allocate time each day to reflect on your responses to challenges and changes. This can help you identify areas for improvement and celebrate successes in practising resilience and adaptability.
- **Mindfulness and Stress Management:** Regular mindfulness practice can enhance both resilience and adaptability by improving emotional regulation and reducing reactivity to stress.
- **Build Support Networks:** Cultivate relationships with individuals who embody resilience and adaptability. These connections can provide support, inspiration, and practical advice when navigating your challenges.

Real-Life Application: Moving Forward with Resilience and Adaptability

As we approach the end of this chapter, it's crucial to recognize that resilience and adaptability are not static qualities but dynamic processes that evolve with our experiences. By applying the strategies discussed and embracing the mindset shifts necessary for growth, we prepare ourselves to face the future with confidence.

The principles of resilience and adaptability have been my compass through times of turmoil and transformation, guiding me from the struggles of my youth in Strabane, through personal and financial adversities, to a place of strength and purpose. Similarly, by embracing these principles, you too can navigate life's uncertainties with grace, turning challenges into opportunities for growth and success.

As we move forward, let us carry the lessons of resilience and adaptability with us, applying them not just in moments of crisis but as integral parts of our approach to life, ensuring we remain flexible, strong, and ready for whatever lies ahead.

Chapter 10: The Principle of Authentic Leadership

Embracing Authenticity for a Fulfilling Life

In the realm of leadership, authenticity isn't just a trait; it's the very cornerstone upon which impactful and enduring leadership is built. Authentic leadership transcends the mere act of guiding others—it's about inspiring, influencing, and instilling trust through genuine interactions and a steadfast commitment to one's values and principles. This chapter delves into the essence of authentic leadership, illustrating its significance through historical examples and drawing on the distilled wisdom of thought leaders to chart a path toward living a life of depth and achievement.

The Historical Pillars of Authentic Leadership

Throughout history, figures who have embodied the principles of authentic leadership have left indelible marks on the world, not just through their accomplishments but through the legacy of their character.

- **Mahatma Gandhi:** Gandhi's leadership in India's struggle for independence was rooted in non-violence and truth. His commitment to his values, even in the face of great personal risk, exemplifies authentic leadership. Gandhi's ability to lead a nation to freedom without veering from his principles of peace and justice showcases how authenticity can galvanize movements and inspire widespread change.
- **Eleanor Roosevelt:** As a champion of human rights,

Roosevelt used her position not for personal gain but to advocate for the marginalized. Her authenticity shone through in her relentless pursuit of equality, her willingness to speak out against injustice, and her ability to connect with people from all walks of life. Roosevelt's leadership was defined by her unwavering integrity and her genuine concern for the welfare of others.

Strategies for Cultivating Authentic Leadership

Authentic leadership is both personal and universal, requiring introspection, a deep understanding of one's values, and the courage to lead by example. Drawing from the collective wisdom of the authors and leaders I've studied, here are key strategies to foster authentic leadership:

- **Know Thyself:** The foundation of authentic leadership lies in self-awareness. Understanding your strengths, weaknesses, values, and motivations is crucial. This self-knowledge not only guides your decisions and actions but also helps you remain true to your principles in the face of challenges.
- **Lead with Vision and Values:** Authentic leaders have a clear vision that is deeply aligned with their values. They communicate this vision with clarity and passion, inspiring others to join them in their pursuit. Leadership is not about wielding power but about empowering others to achieve a common goal.
- **Build Genuine Relationships:** Authentic leadership

is characterized by sincere, meaningful connections. It's about listening, showing empathy, and valuing the contributions of others. By fostering an environment of trust and respect, authentic leaders create a culture where everyone feels valued and motivated to contribute their best.

- **Practice Resilience and Adaptability:** Authentic leaders are resilient, and capable of navigating adversity while staying true to their values. They also possess the adaptability to respond to changing circumstances with creativity and grace. This combination of resilience and adaptability allows them to lead effectively through uncertainty.

Authentic Leadership for a Life Well-Lived

Adopting authentic leadership principles is about more than achieving professional success; it's a pathway to "getting a life" that is rich in purpose, fulfilment, and genuine connections. By leading authentically, we not only inspire those around us but also cultivate a life that is aligned with our deepest values and aspirations.

In embracing the principle of authentic leadership, we commit to continuous growth, integrity, and positive influence. This commitment not only shapes our legacy but also ensures that our leadership is a true reflection of who we are, inviting others to pursue their dreams with authenticity and courage.

Continuing from the foundational aspects of authentic leadership, we explore further how to integrate these principles into daily practice, ensuring they resonate through our personal and professional lives. Authentic leadership is not a static achievement but a dynamic process of growth, reflection, and action. It's about making a conscious decision every day to lead with integrity, empathy, and a deep commitment to positive impact.

Living Authentically: Beyond the Office

Authentic leadership extends beyond the confines of professional settings into every facet of our lives. It's about how we interact with our family, friends, and community, and how we handle personal challenges and successes.

- **Consistency in Values:** Authenticity requires that our values are consistent across all areas of our lives. This congruence ensures that our actions, regardless of the setting, reflect our true selves and what we stand for. It's this consistency that builds trust and credibility, both of which are essential for effective leadership.

- **Vulnerability as Strength:** Authentic leaders embrace vulnerability. Sharing our challenges, doubts, and fears doesn't weaken our leadership; it humanizes us and fosters deeper connections. Vulnerability encourages openness and mutual support within teams and relationships, creating a stronger, more cohesive unit.

Empowering Others: The Mark of an Authentic Leader

One of the most powerful aspects of authentic leadership is the emphasis on empowering others. Authentic leaders recognize their role in developing the potential of those around them, encouraging growth, learning, and independence.

- **Mentorship and Development:** Taking an active interest in the development of others is a hallmark of authentic leadership. This can involve mentoring, providing opportunities for growth, and encouraging continuous learning. By investing in the development of others, we not only contribute to their success but also to the creation of a culture of learning and empowerment.

- **Fostering a Safe Environment for Risk-taking:** Authentic leaders create environments where taking calculated risks is encouraged. They understand that innovation and growth often require stepping out of their comfort zones. By supporting risk-taking and viewing failures as learning opportunities, authentic leaders cultivate an atmosphere of trust and innovation.

Adaptability in Leadership

Authentic leadership also involves adaptability – the ability to adjust one's leadership style and strategies to meet the needs of the situation or the individuals being led. This flexibility does not mean compromising on values but rather applying them in ways that are most effective in each unique context.

- **Listening and Learning:** Authentic leaders are attentive listeners and are open to learning from others, regardless of their position. This openness to new ideas and feedback is crucial for adaptability, allowing leaders to make informed decisions and adjustments as needed.

- **Embracing Change:** Change is a constant, and authentic leaders embrace it as an opportunity for growth and improvement. They lead by example, navigating changes with a positive attitude and a clear vision, and inspiring others to approach change with an open mind.

Real-World Application: Leading Authentically in Diverse Settings

By working in various leadership roles across different industries I have learned the importance of applying authentic leadership principles universally. By staying true to my values, even when it meant walking away from opportunities that didn't align with them, I demonstrated the importance of integrity in leadership.

Leading from the front, especially in achieving top sales positions, was not just about personal success but about showing what's possible through hard work, dedication, and a genuine approach to serving customers and supporting team members.

Strategies for Cultivating Authentic Leadership

Developing into an authentic leader involves continuous self-reflection, practice, and commitment to personal growth. Here are actionable strategies to cultivate authentic leadership:

- **Regular Self-Assessment:** Regularly evaluate your

leadership style, decisions, and actions against your core values and principles. This ongoing self-assessment helps ensure alignment between your beliefs and your leadership approach.

- **Seek Diverse Perspectives:** Surround yourself with a diverse range of voices and perspectives. This diversity enriches your understanding and approach to leadership, helping you to lead more effectively in varied contexts.
- **Commit to Transparency:** Practice transparency in your decision-making and communications. Transparency builds trust and demonstrates integrity, both of which are critical for authentic leadership.

As we conclude this section of the chapter on Authentic Leadership, remember that becoming an authentic leader is both personal and perpetual. It's a path marked by self-discovery, integrity, and a profound commitment to positively influencing those around us. By embracing the principles of authentic leadership, we unlock the potential to not only achieve professional success but also to lead a life that is truly fulfilling and aligned with our deepest values.

Cultivating a Culture of Authenticity

An authentic leader's influence extends beyond individual interactions; it seeds a culture of authenticity within the organization or community they lead. This culture encourages honesty, integrity, and genuine connection, fostering an environment where everyone feels valued and empowered to contribute their best.

- **Encourage Open Dialogue:** Create channels for open, honest communication. Encourage team members to share their ideas, concerns, and feedback without fear of judgment or retribution. This openness not only builds trust but also enriches the decision-making process with diverse perspectives.
- **Lead with Empathy:** Understanding and empathizing with the experiences and challenges of those you lead is crucial. It involves active listening, acknowledging others' feelings, and responding with compassion and support. Empathy strengthens relationships and builds a supportive, cohesive team.

Overcoming Challenges to Authentic Leadership

While the road to authentic leadership is rewarding, it's not without its challenges. Navigating scepticism, resistance, or misunderstanding requires resilience, patience, and a steadfast commitment to your principles.

- **Stay True to Your Values:** In the face of challenges or opposition, it's essential to remain anchored to your values. This consistency reinforces your authenticity and helps navigate difficult situations with integrity.
- **Adapt and Innovate:** Encountering resistance is an opportunity to adapt and innovate. It invites you to explore new approaches and solutions that align with your authentic leadership style while addressing the concerns or needs of those you lead.

Personal Reflections and Future Directions

Reflecting on my life, the decision to align my professional life with my values, lead by example, and prioritize the development and empowerment of others has not only defined my leadership style but also enriched my personal life. Authentic leadership is a continuous journey of growth, learning, and adaptation.

- **Commit to Lifelong Learning:** Embrace the mindset of a lifelong learner. Continuously seek opportunities to expand your knowledge, skills, and understanding of leadership and the world around you.
- **Build a Support Network:** Surround yourself with mentors, peers, and advisors who embody authentic leadership. This network can provide guidance, support, and inspiration as you navigate your growth in leadership.
- **Reflect and Adjust:** Regular reflection is key to authentic leadership. Take time to assess your actions, decisions, and their impact. Be open to feedback and willing to make adjustments to ensure your leadership remains authentic and effective.

Conclusion: Embodying Authentic Leadership

As we conclude this exploration of the Principle of Authentic Leadership, remember that being an authentic leader is about much more than achieving professional success. It's about leading a life that is true to your values, inspiring and empowering those around you, and making a positive impact in the world.

It is a voyage filled with opportunities for growth, challenges to overcome, and the potential to inspire change. By embracing your authentic self, leading with integrity and empathy, and committing to the continuous development of yourself and those you lead, you pave the way for a fulfilling life and legacy defined by genuine leadership and positive influence.

Let this chapter not only serve as a guide but also as an inspiration to embrace the principles of authentic leadership and that it will help you "get a life" that is rich in purpose, connection, and achievement.

Chapter 11: The Principle of The Power of Belief and Faith

Faith and Belief

As we embark on this chapter, it's important to clarify that my focus will be on the concepts of belief and faith, distinct from the specifics of organized religion. My wife and I hail from diverse religious traditions, yet we share a profound connection through our deep-seated beliefs and faith. In my view, we are all engaging with the same universal force, albeit through different 'service providers.' This perspective fosters a deep respect for the myriad ways individuals express and practice their faith across the globe.

In the landscape of life's principles, the power of belief and faith emerges as a profound force, shaping our destinies and colouring our worldviews. This chapter delves into the essence of these forces as foundational elements for personal empowerment, resilience, and purposeful living.

Through personal anecdotes and broader reflections, we explore how deep-seated belief and unwavering faith in oneself and one's values can illuminate the path to "getting a life" that is not only fulfilling but also impactful.

Rooted in Tradition, Reaching for the Universal

Growing up in Ireland, the weekly ritual of Catholic mass instilled in me a sense of community, tradition, and a connection to something greater than myself. The fact that my father was a Funeral Director also brought life, death and traditions to the forefront of my mind regularly. These early experiences laid the groundwork for an understanding of faith as both a personal voyage and a collective endeavour.

In parallel, my wife's spiritual odyssey, rooted in her Presbyterian/Methodist heritage in Belfast, took her on a voyage of profound commitment and service. Her decision to attend Bible college and dedicate seven years of her life as a Christian missionary in Tanzania speaks to the incredible strength and direction that faith can provide. Her journey exemplifies faith in action—living out one's beliefs through service, compassion, and a deep commitment to making a tangible difference in the lives of others.

The Transformative Power of Belief and Faith

Belief and faith transcend the boundaries of religious practices to touch upon the very core of our being. They are about trusting in the unseen, holding onto hope in the face of adversity, and believing in our ability to overcome and thrive. The authors and thought leaders I've studied have consistently highlighted faith and belief not only as spiritual concepts but as universal principles of human resilience and potential.

- **Belief as the Foundation for Action:** Belief in oneself, in the potential for change, and in the possibility of achieving one's dreams acts as a powerful motivator. It propels us forward, turning aspirations into actions and visions into realities.
- **Faith as the Bedrock of Resilience:** Faith provides a steady anchor in the tumultuous seas of life. Whether derived from religious convictions or a secular sense of trust in the unfolding journey of life, faith imbues us with the strength to face challenges with hope and

perseverance.

Living Faith: Personal Stories of Belief in Action

The narrative of my upbringing in Donegal, coupled with my wife's transformative experience in Tanzania, underscores the multifaceted nature of faith. These stories highlight faith not as a mere abstract concept but as a lived reality, guiding decisions, inspiring service, and fostering a life of deep, meaningful engagement with the world.

- **Embracing Diversity:** Our distinct faiths reveal the rich tapestry of belief systems that inform and shape our lives. From Catholic mass and funerals in Donegal to the mission fields of Tanzania, faith in its many expressions drives us to seek connection, understanding, and a way to contribute positively to the world around us.

- **The Ripple Effect of Faithful Living:** The decision to align one's life with deeply held beliefs and to act on those convictions has a ripple effect, touching the lives of those around us and inspiring others to explore their paths of belief and action.

Harnessing the Power of Belief and Faith

To tap into the transformative power of belief and faith, we must first acknowledge their centrality in our lives and then consciously integrate them into our daily actions and decisions. This integration involves:

- **Cultivating Self-Belief:** Recognizing and nurturing

belief in our capabilities and worth is essential for overcoming obstacles and pursuing our goals with confidence.

- **Living Your Faith:** Whether through religious practice, community service, or personal reflection, actively living out your faith ensures that your beliefs are not static but dynamic forces that shape your interactions with the world.

- **Embracing Challenges as Opportunities for Growth:** Viewing challenges through the lens of faith and belief enables us to approach them not as insurmountable barriers but as opportunities for growth, learning, and deepening our resilience.

As we embark on this exploration of belief and faith, let us remember that these principles offer more than comfort; they provide a framework for action, a source of strength, and a beacon of hope. By delving into our beliefs and nurturing our faith, we unlock the potential to lead lives of profound meaning, purpose, and impact.

Broadening the Spectrum of Belief and Faith

Faith, whether rooted in religious tradition or personal conviction, underscores a universal truth: belief and faith are potent drivers of human action and resilience. My wife's dedication in Africa exemplifies the manifestations of faith and its capacity to inspire service, commitment, and transformation. This serves, not only to highlight the personal nature of faith but also its universal power to motivate and guide.

Integrating Faith into Daily Life

Incorporating the essence of belief and faith into our daily existence enhances our ability to face challenges with confidence and to live authentically according to our values. This integration involves several key practices:

- **Reflective Practice:** Regular reflection on one's beliefs and how they align with daily actions fosters a deeper connection with one's faith. This can be facilitated through meditation, prayer, journaling, or contemplative walks, providing space to contemplate our spiritual journey and its reflection in our lives.
- **Community Engagement:** Engaging with a community that shares or supports your faith and beliefs can reinforce your sense of purpose and provide a network of support and encouragement. Community can be found in religious congregations, spiritual groups, or social circles that value deep, meaningful conversations about life's big questions.
- **Service and Action:** Faith becomes most vivid when put into action. Volunteering, community service, or simple acts of kindness are practical expressions of belief and faith. These actions reinforce our commitment to our values and the impact we wish to have on the world.

Challenges to Belief and Faith

While belief and faith can be sources of immense strength, they are not without challenges. Doubt, external skepticism, and internal conflicts can test our convictions. Navigating these challenges requires resilience and a willingness to explore and question deeply.

- **Embracing Doubt as Part of Faith:** Doubt is not antithetical to faith but a component of its growth. Facing and wrestling with doubts can lead to a more profound, considered faith. It's through questioning that we often find deeper understanding and reaffirmation of our beliefs.
- **Seeking Wisdom and Guidance:** In times of uncertainty or conflict, turning to trusted sources of wisdom—be it religious texts, spiritual leaders, or personal mentors—can provide clarity and reassurance. The insights of others, combined with our reflections, can guide us through periods of doubt or reevaluation.

Stories of Resilience Through Faith

Beyond personal anecdotes, history and contemporary life brim with stories of individuals and communities whose faith propelled them to remarkable acts of resilience, courage, and transformation.

- **Community Resilience:** Consider the communities worldwide that have faced adversity, from natural disasters to social injustices. The shared faith within these communities—whether spiritual or a collective belief in their cause—has often been the catalyst for rebuilding, reform, and hope amidst despair.
- **Inspirational Leaders:** Leaders who've harnessed

their faith as a source of strength and guidance, using it to inspire movements, challenge injustices, and foster peace, remind us of the transformative power of belief. Their lives encourage us to explore how our faith can inform our leadership and impact.

Cultivating a Personal Philosophy of Faith

Developing a personal philosophy of faith that guides your life and actions involves ongoing exploration, commitment, and openness to growth. This philosophy becomes your compass, guiding decisions, influencing how you interact with the world, and shaping the legacy you aim to leave.

- **Articulate Your Beliefs:** Take time to articulate what you believe and why. This process can help clarify your values and how they intersect with your faith.

- **Live Intentionally According to Your Faith:** Ensure your life's choices—from your career to your relationships and daily habits—reflect your faith and beliefs. This congruence between belief and action breeds authenticity and fulfilment.

- **Share and Inspire:** Sharing your experiences of faith and belief, with their ups and downs, can inspire others. Whether through writing, speaking, or simply living by example, your story can be a beacon for others exploring their beliefs.

Conclusion: The Enduring Power of Belief and Faith

As we conclude this exploration of the Principle of The Power of Belief and Faith, it's clear that these forces are much more than personal convictions—they're the underpinnings of a life lived with purpose, resilience, and impact. By embracing and nurturing our beliefs and faith, we open ourselves to a life of deeper meaning, guiding us to "get a life" that transcends the ordinary and touches the extraordinary.

Let this chapter serve not only as a reflection on the power of belief and faith but as an invitation to weave these principles into the fabric of your life, empowering you to face challenges with strength, live with purpose, and influence the world positively.

Chapter 12: The Principle of Legacy and Impact

Moving on to Chapter 12 we delve into a principle profoundly intertwined with the essence of our existence and the marks we leave behind—The Principle of Legacy and Impact. This exploration is not just about the material or the tangible but delves deeper into the values, actions, and essence that we bequeath to future generations. As a father and a husband, the contemplation of legacy holds a special place in my heart, guiding my actions and aspirations with the hope of leaving a meaningful imprint for my children, Caogain, Jimmy, Emily, and Bryony, and beyond.

Legacy: Beyond the Material

The concept of legacy often conjures images of wealth and possessions passed down through family lines. However, its true significance lies far deeper, in the lessons taught, the love shared, and the examples set. It's the invisible threads of moral fibre, resilience, and kindness that weave through the fabric of our communities, shaping a future long after we're gone.

For me, the importance of creating a legacy that resonates with integrity, compassion, and a deep-seated respect for others was instilled early on, growing up amidst the verdant landscapes of Ireland. The weekly tradition of attending Catholic mass with my family not only grounded me in a community of faith but also instilled in me the values of perseverance, community support, and a commitment to something greater than oneself. These experiences have been pivotal in shaping my understanding of the impact one's life can have on others and the world at large.

The Interplay of Diverse Faiths in Shaping Legacy

Enhancing the depth of my own Catholic experience, my wife's Protestant heritage from Belfast and her heartfelt commitment as a Christian missionary in Africa beautifully demonstrates the powerful influence of faith and belief in shaping our choices and guiding our decisions. Her unwavering dedication to serving others, rooted in a profound sense of faith, exemplifies the remarkable difference one person, fuelled by genuine conviction and a sincere wish to contribute positively, can make in the world.

This melding of our backgrounds and beliefs serves as a living example for our children—Caogain, Jimmy, Emily, and Bryony—demonstrating that legacy is not merely about what we leave behind but how we live our lives and the principles we stand for. It underscores the importance of living a life that is not only true to one's beliefs but also actively contributes to the well-being of others and the world at large.

Reflecting on the Impact of Our Actions

As we contemplate the legacy we wish to leave, it becomes imperative to reflect on the daily actions and choices that contribute to this lasting imprint. Each decision, interaction, and endeavour carries with it the potential to affect change, inspire others, and lay a path that others may follow. It prompts us to ask ourselves:

- How do my actions reflect the values I wish to pass on?
- In what ways am I contributing to the world and the

communities I am part of?

- What example am I setting for my children, and how will this shape the legacy I leave behind?

Cultivating a Legacy Through Intentional Living

Living with the end in mind encourages us to lead lives of intention, purpose, and impact. It's about aligning our daily choices with the broader vision we have for our legacy—ensuring that our time here contributes to a positive, lasting change that will benefit not just the present but future generations.

For those of us navigating the complexities of parenthood, career, and personal aspirations, the concept of legacy offers a guiding light, helping to prioritize what truly matters. It's a reminder that our greatest achievements may not always be measured in accolades or wealth but in the love we share, the lives we touch, and the world we help to shape for the better.

As we delve deeper into this exploration of legacy and impact, let us keep at the forefront the profound responsibility and opportunity we have to influence the future through our actions today. This initial foray into the Principle of Legacy and Impact sets the stage for a deeper exploration of how we can each cultivate a legacy that resonates with meaning, purpose, and positive transformation, not just for our immediate family but for the world at large.

Continuing our exploration of the Principle of Legacy and Impact, we delve into practical ways to embody these values in our daily lives, ensuring our actions resonate with the legacy we aspire to leave. This involves a conscious effort to live intentionally, making decisions that align with our deepest values and striving to make a positive impact on those around us and the broader world.

Living Intentionally for Impact

To live a life that aligns with the legacy we wish to leave, we must adopt a mindset of intentional living. This means making choices that are reflective of our core values and the impact we hope to have. It's about being mindful of how our everyday actions contribute to the broader tapestry of our legacy.

- **Mindfulness in Daily Decisions:** Every choice, from the way we communicate with others to the projects we undertake, is a building block of our legacy. By being mindful of the implications of our decisions, we can ensure they contribute positively to the legacy we aim to build.

- **Purposeful Actions:** Align your actions with your purpose. Whether it's through your career, volunteer work, or personal projects, find ways to infuse your daily life with actions that reflect your core values and contribute to the greater good.

The Role of Relationships in Shaping Legacy

Our relationships play a crucial role in the legacy we leave behind. The way we interact with family, friends, colleagues, and even strangers can have a lasting impact, influencing how we're remembered and the influence we've had on others' lives.

- **Nurturing Meaningful Connections:** Invest time and effort into building and maintaining relationships that are meaningful and enriching.

These connections not only support us through life but also amplify our ability to make a positive impact.

- **Teaching and Learning:** Our interactions with others are opportunities for mutual growth. By teaching, sharing, and learning, we contribute to a legacy of knowledge and wisdom that can guide future generations.

Reflective Practices for Legacy Building

Developing a clear vision of the legacy we want to leave requires reflection and thoughtful consideration. Engaging in reflective practices can help clarify our values, aspirations, and the mark we wish to make on the world.

- **Journaling:** Regularly writing down your thoughts, experiences, and reflections can offer insights into the values and principles most important to you. This practice can help crystallize your vision for the legacy you wish to leave.
- **Legacy Letters:** Consider writing legacy letters to your loved ones. These letters can express your values, hopes, and the lessons you wish to pass on, serving as a tangible part of your legacy.

Making a Difference Through Service

Service to others is one of the most profound ways to build a meaningful legacy. By dedicating our time, resources, and talents to causes and initiatives that align with our values, we can make a tangible impact on the world and inspire others to do the same.

- **Volunteering:** Engage in volunteer work that resonates with your passions and values. This not only contributes to your community but also sets an example of service and generosity for others to follow.
- **Advocacy and Activism:** Use your voice and platform to advocate for causes you believe in. Championing social, environmental, or economic initiatives can be a powerful component of your legacy, driving change and inspiring action.

As we continue to explore the Principle of Legacy and Impact, it becomes evident that the legacy we leave is deeply intertwined with the lives we lead each day. By living intentionally, nurturing relationships, engaging in reflective practices, and serving others, we lay the foundation for a legacy that transcends material possessions, reflecting instead a life of purpose, impact, and positive change. Our actions today are the seeds of the legacy we leave for future generations, including our children and their children. Let us strive to make each action count, building a legacy that not only reflects our deepest values but also contributes to a better world for those who follow.

As we draw closer to the conclusion of our exploration into the Principle of Legacy and Impact, it's crucial to recognize that creating a meaningful legacy is both a personal and collective endeavour. It requires us to look beyond our immediate concerns and consider the broader implications of our actions. This final segment aims to provide actionable insights and reflections to help solidify our understanding of how to live in a way that ensures our legacy is both impactful and enduring.

Cultivating a Legacy Mindset

Adopting a legacy mindset means seeing beyond the horizon of our lifetimes, and understanding that our actions today ripple through time, affecting generations to come. For us, it's about making conscious choices that reflect the kind of world we want to leave behind for our children, Caogain, Jimmy, Emily, and Bryony, and their descendants.

- **Sustainability and Stewardship:** In every decision, consider the sustainability of your actions and their impact on the environment and society. Whether it's reducing waste, supporting renewable energy, or engaging in community clean-up efforts, small changes can contribute to a healthier planet for future generations.
- **Ethical Living:** Strive to live ethically, making choices that reflect fairness, integrity, and respect for others. By embodying these values, you inspire those around you to do the same, creating a ripple effect that enhances your legacy.

Passing on Values through Stories and Traditions

One of the most powerful ways to ensure the longevity of your values and beliefs is through the sharing of stories and the establishment of meaningful traditions. These narratives and rituals become the vessels through which your legacy is passed down, imbuing future generations with a sense of identity, belonging, and purpose.

- **Share Your Journey:** Regularly share stories of your life's challenges, triumphs, and lessons learned with your children and loved ones. These stories humanize you, making the values you lived by more tangible and relatable to those who follow.
- **Create Meaningful Traditions:** Establish family traditions that reflect your values and beliefs. Whether it's volunteering together as a family, participating in cultural rituals, or simply gathering for regular family meals, these traditions reinforce the principles you hold dear.

Legacy as an Ongoing Process

Building a legacy is not a one-time event but an ongoing process that evolves with our lives. It's about continually assessing our actions and their alignment with the legacy we wish to create, making adjustments as necessary to ensure our impact remains positive and aligned with our core values.

- **Continuous Reflection and Reevaluation:** Regularly take time to reflect on your legacy and its current trajectory. Are your actions still aligned with the values you wish to pass on? What changes or improvements can be made?
- **Encourage Active Participation:** Involve your family, especially your children, in discussions about

legacy and impact. Encourage them to think about the values they wish to live by and the legacy they want to create. This not only empowers them but also ensures the continuation of a legacy mindset across generations.

The Legacy We Leave

As we conclude this chapter on the Principle of Legacy and Impact, let us be reminded that the true measure of our lives is not found in material success or accolades but in the positive impact we have on the lives of others and the world we leave behind. Our legacy is crafted daily through our actions, decisions, and the values we embody. By living intentionally, with a focus on sustainability, ethical behaviour, and the sharing of our stories and traditions, we create a legacy that endures, inspiring future generations to continue the work of making the world a better place.

Let this exploration of legacy and impact serve not only as a reflection on the importance of the marks we leave behind but also as a call to action to live each day with purpose and intention. Our legacy is the gift we give to the future, a testament to our existence and the values we've championed. In the end, it's through our legacy that we achieve immortality, living on in the hearts and minds of those we've touched and the positive changes we've instigated in the world.

Chapter 13 – The Way Forward

Embarking on the final chapter of "Get A Life," I aim to distil the essence and key messages of the principles we have explored. My goal is to inspire hope and confidence that living by these principles is not only possible but can indeed lead to profound change and fulfilment.

The Essence of Transformation

At the heart of this book lies a simple yet profound truth: the quality of our lives is directly shaped by the principles we choose to live by. From cultivating a mindset of growth and resilience to embracing authentic leadership and leaving a lasting legacy, each principle offers a pathway to a life of deeper meaning, purpose, and joy.

As we reflect on these teachings, it's important to recognize that "getting the life you really want" is both unique and universal—unique in that each of us will navigate our lives in our own way, and universal in that the principles themselves apply to all, regardless of our individual circumstances or aspirations.

Living the Principles: A Personal Commitment

For me, the commitment to living according to these principles is not merely theoretical but a daily practice. Do I fail to achieve them all every day? Definitely! Do I keep going anyway, and try to be 1% better tomorrow? Absolutely! As long as we are trying, we are doing better than 90% of the population who have no compass or plan.

Getting a Life involves continuous reflection, intentional action, and an openness to learning and growth. As I look to the future, my resolve to embody these principles in every aspect of my life remains unwavering. This commitment is driven by a deep-seated belief in their power to effect genuine change, not just within myself, but in the world around me.

- **Growth and Resilience:** I will continue to embrace challenges as opportunities for growth, viewing setbacks not as defeats but as lessons that strengthen my resilience and propel me forward.
- **Authentic Leadership:** Leading by example, I will strive to maintain integrity, empathy, and transparency in my interactions, inspiring those around me to pursue their own paths with authenticity and courage.
- **Legacy and Impact:** Mindful of the legacy I wish to leave, I will endeavour to make choices that reflect my values, contribute positively to my community, and encourage a better future for the next generations.

Principles in Practice

As you move towards "getting the life you really want," I offer these principles not as rigid rules but as guiding lights. Each principle, when applied with intention and consistency, can open doors to new possibilities, deeper fulfilment, and lasting change.

- **Start Small, Think Big:** Begin by implementing small changes that align with these principles. Over time, these small steps will accumulate, leading to significant transformations in your life and the lives of those around you.

- **Reflect and Adapt:** Regularly take time to reflect on your progress, challenges, and the alignment of your actions with your goals. Be prepared to adapt your strategies, knowing that flexibility and resilience are key to overcoming obstacles and staying on course.
- **Seek Support and Community:** Remember, you are not alone. Seek out mentors, peers, and communities that share your values and aspirations. Together, we can support each other, share insights, and celebrate successes.

A Message of Empowerment

As we draw to a close, it's time to reflect on what we have learned. The essence of our exploration was to illuminate the possibility that resides within each of us to transform our lives through the power of intentional living, guided by timeless principles that have shaped the lives of many before us.

Embracing What Lies Ahead

As we stand on the brink of new beginnings, armed with knowledge and insights, it's crucial to acknowledge that the journey does not end here. The principles we've delved into are not checkboxes to tick off but seeds to plant, nurture, and grow throughout the entirety of our lives.

"Get A Life" was conceived as a blueprint for living—a dynamic, evolving guide adaptable to the unique contours of each individual's life. As you go get your life, remember that the principles laid out are not prescriptive but suggestive, inviting you to interpret and apply them in ways that resonate most deeply with your aspirations and circumstances.

Final Words

To every reader who has accompanied me, thank you. Your willingness to explore, reflect, and embrace the possibility of transformation is the first step toward realizing the life you envision. My hope is that this book serves as a beacon, illuminating your path as you navigate the complexities and joys of life.

May you move forward with the courage to implement these principles, the resilience to weather the storms, and the conviction to build a legacy of positive impact. Remember, the life YOU really want is within your grasp—shaped by your beliefs, your actions, and your unwavering commitment to growth and purpose.

Let us step into the future with hope, empowered by the knowledge that we have the tools and the capacity to create a life of profound meaning and joy. Together, let's "Get A Life" we truly want, one filled with purpose, fulfilment, and lasting happiness.

The 12 Get A Life Principles and Their Influences.

1. **Growth Mindset**: Inspired by the works of James Clear ("Atomic Habits"), emphasizing small changes for massive growth.
2. **Resilience**: Drawing on Dr. Wayne W. Dyer's teachings on seeing obstacles as opportunities for growth.
3. **Authenticity**: Echoing the philosophies of Ralph Waldo Emerson and his emphasis on individuality and personal integrity.
4. **Leadership**: John C. Maxwell's insights on leadership

as an act of influence and empowerment.

5. **Legacy**: Inspired by the life lessons and teachings of Tony Robbins, focusing on living with purpose and creating a lasting impact.

6. **Impact**: The work of authors like Simon Sinek, on finding one's "Why" and making a difference.

7. **Continuous Learning**: Emphasized across the works of many thought leaders, including Brian Tracy's focus on self-development and mastery.

8. **Mindfulness and Gratitude**: Themes explored by Dr. Joseph Murphy and within James Allen's works, highlight the power of positive thinking and gratitude.

9. **Service**: The life and teachings of figures like Mother Teresa, are reflected in the compassionate service ethos of authors like Bob Proctor and Les Brown.

10. **Financial Intelligence**: Directly tied to George S. Clason ("The Richest Man in Babylon") and Robert Kiyosaki ("Rich Dad Poor Dad") for their foundational financial wisdom.

11. **Goal Setting and Visualization**: Techniques and strategies advocated by Tony Robbins, emphasise the clarity of vision and the power of setting achievable goals.

12. **Personal Power and Action**: Tony Robbins' work on unleashing one's potential to achieve extraordinary results, embodying the principles of personal power and proactive action.

Also by Brian McGinty

Unleashing Your Infinite Potential
Get A Life - Get The Life You Really Want

Watch for more at https://getalife.info.

About the Author

Happy husband and father of four. Mentor, Consultant, Author, and world explorer.

Read more at https://getalife.info.

ACKNOWLEDGMENTS

I want to dedicate this to my team that helps me behind the scenes, from my editors, test readers, graphic designers, and the list goes on. Truly appreciate each of you for keeping me on my toes.